The Oshun Diaries

Encounters with an African Goddess

Diane Esguerra

EYE BOOKS
NON-FICTION

Published by Eye Books
29A Barrow Street
Much Wenlock
Shropshire
TF13 6EN

www.eye-books.com

First edition 2019
Copyright © Diane Esguerra 2019
Cover design by Sophie Pasiewicz and Sally Crombie

British Library Cataloguing in Publication Data
A catalogue record for this book is available from the British Library

Printed by CPI Group (UK) Ltd, Croydon CR0 4YY

ISBN 9781785631474

For David
My first reader – always

No one can hope to create a lasting structure. What I can offer is to provide a brief glimpse of this immense world for others; like a vast landscape at night, lit up for a fraction of a second by lightning. The creation of the world happens continuously. Everything dies into a new birth.

Adunni Olorisha

The twenty-first century will be the century of Africa.
Those who suffer most earn the right to the greatest happiness.
Learn from Africa! Follow Africa!
Only then will the world change, will the new dawn of humanism come.

Daisaku Ikeda

Contents

Part 2 – America: The Sacred Orisha Gardens

Introduction

I CAN SEE her out of the corner of my eye, slouching against the window, her elongated face etched with sadness. Those heavy-lidded eyes of hers stare at me, reproachfully.

Guilty, once again, of neglect, I fetch a rag and a bottle of extra-virgin olive oil from the kitchen. I lay her gently on top of last week's newspapers. Starting with her hexagonal top-knot I slowly make my way down her skinny, cinnamon body, rubbing oil into pouting lips, pointy breasts, twerky buttocks, and bandy legs which hover above tiny, shoeless feet. Trickiest of all to oil are her slender fingers which clutch a bag of cowry shells, and, hidden beneath the beaded waistband, her secret female places. After all these years she and I have grown to know each other pretty well.

She never wanted to come here in the first place.

'Bin twice round the world', the British Airways courier announced when he dumped her on my Brighton doorstep twenty years ago.

'Thank-you so much, I'd given up hope of ever seeing her

again. She's been missing for seventeen days now.'

'Yeah, completely lost track of this one, we did. Gave them a laugh in Missing Cargo though…told me they'd never lost a goddess before!'

She'd only just fitted into the trunk I'd bought especially for her and her alone; all 111 centimetres of her hardwood self. Her base, which bore the name of the sculptor and master woodcarver who created her – Kasali – was bashed about a bit, but to my relief she herself remained unblemished.

In Oshun State, Nigeria, a region famous for growing indigo and using it as a dye, I'd selected her from Kasali's litter of hand-carved Yoruba gods. Outside his humble studio shack close to the Sacred Groves of Oshogbo, Kasali explained that he was, in fact, *Arelagbayi*: born into a family which hands down from generation to generation the sacred craft of carving images of the gods of the Yoruba – black Africa's largest ethnic group.

Fixing me with his gaze he told me that the spirit of the goddess Oshun had possessed him during the process of carving this particular image.

'We all born child of one *orisha*. Oshun – she your goddess now,' Kasali said, handing her to me with tender reverence. 'It good give her many offering. She get plenty power.'

Three days later Oshun and I checked in at Murtala Mohammed airport in Lagos. And ten hours after that, with a sinking heart and kicking myself for not bothering with travel insurance, I'd waited, in vain, for her to appear on the Heathrow luggage carousel. Believing I'd lost her for seventeen days certainly helped me value her more. Perhaps that is what she'd intended all along.

Suitably oiled and shiny once again, I return the tardy goddess to her corner of the room. Above her hangs a small watercolour painted by my sister, Sally, an artist, in honour of

Oshun's eventual arrival on these shores all those years ago: a fat, black woman, her arms outstretched, is flying through the third-floor arched window of our Victorian apartment and into our living room. Beneath her red, billowing dress Sally had scrawled *Mammy Water Visits Brighton*.

The goddess continues to stare at me sulkily. We both know she'd rather be elsewhere. The Caribbean, Latin America, Cuba, Brazil – maybe even the States. Anywhere that she would be suitably venerated. Anywhere, in fact, bar cold, old colonialist England. Best of all, I know she'd rather be back home in Africa.

I consider Kasali's suggestion of an offering. If I were to lay something indigo-coloured at her feet to remind her of home…a bunch of agapanthus, perhaps – or even a scrap of denim. I decide, in the end, to place her next to my Buddhist altar. Indigo is mentioned in the writings of Nichiren Daishonin, the 13th-century Japanese Buddhist priest whose teachings I follow: *If one dyes something repeatedly in indigo, it becomes even bluer than the indigo leaves. The Lotus Sutra is like the indigo, and the strength of one's practice is like the deepening blue.* The Japanese god of *ai* (indigo) is called Aizen Shin and the spoken word *ai* means both indigo and love. Oshun is, after all, a goddess of love. It could, likewise, be said that the deeper you penetrate the mysteries of this energy known as Oshun the more intensely her fierce uniqueness shines through.

As mesmerising as she is, Kasali's wooden image of Oshun is a mere simulacrum of the real thing. Years before I acquired her I'd had a surprise, fleeting encounter with the goddess herself.

But I hadn't travelled to her Oshogbo birthplace that first time with the intention of seeking out Oshun; I'd ventured there in the hope of meeting someone else.

Part 1

Africa:
The Sacred Groves

Oshogbo

MEMORY is visceral. All I can recall, about the drive into the southern Nigerian town of Oshogbo that November afternoon in 1986, is the screech of worn tyres on khaki-coloured roads, the all-pervading dust, the torrid heat and the rivulets of sweat trickling down the back of the albino driver's neck. After the 150-mile drive from Lagos on a gridlocked highway I was desperately thirsty and dying for a pee. So intent was I on finding somewhere to satisfy my bodily needs that I scarcely took in my surroundings. Victorian explorer Henry M Stanley used 'dark' in the title of his book *Through the Dark Continent* to describe that which is mysterious and unknown. Little did I realise, that day, that this would be the start of my journey into a dark, hidden Africa.

Pulling up outside her home – if you could call it a home – was a different matter. After all these years the image of that baroque, semi-dilapidated, Portuguese-colonial edifice, with alien-like carvings clinging to its walls, remains soldered to my brain.

Something in me hesitated before knocking on her front door; a crisis of confidence, I suppose. I'd given no thought as to how I was going to present myself to the woman I'd travelled all this distance to meet. As an English writer and performance artist with a keen interest in anthropology? The ex-wife of an architect working in Lagos? The truth of the matter is that on that first visit my motive for wanting to meet her was essentially a monetary one. I was broke. I hoped that this woman whose door I was now banging on would be a worthy enough subject to merit a documentary proposal.

'Come away. Your persistence may anger her,' Ebis advised, leading me gently back to the car. 'Let us take some refreshment and return later.'

In the windowless, earthen-floored bar with its ineffective plastic fly-screen and unwiped tables we sipped Fanta and chewed on stale Lincoln biscuits.

I let out a sigh. 'I can't believe I've come all this way for nothing.'

Ebis smiled. 'No journey is ever wasted.'

We hadn't known each other long. A Nigerian radio journalist and DJ, Ebis had offered to accompany me on this recce to Oshogbo, and had helped me hire our driver and his rusty Peugeot. A year or two older than I, the handsome, gap-toothed young man had once been a Christian preacher – until the desire to expose corruption in public office and the lure of African Reggae had proved too irresistible. He'd interviewed me the week before about the forthcoming production of my play at Nigeria's National Theatre in Lagos. We'd hit it off immediately.

'If it weren't for the bloody British Council,' I grumbled, 'I wouldn't be here today.' Much to my annoyance and that of the theatre, the British Council in Lagos, which had initially expressed a keen interest in backing the play, had now decided they didn't want to have anything to do with it. We'd been depending on their support. Production money was scarce and I knew if the play were to go ahead I'd earn peanuts. The BBC script unit had recently expressed an interest in any proposals I could come up with – including documentary ones. I was eager to have a project up my sleeve to take back to England.

Ebis and I were sharing a second bottle of Fanta when a young man in a striped *agbada* strolled into the bar. He stared at us for a few moments and then walked over to our table.

'Excuse me. I saw you outside the house in Ibokun Road. I know whom you are seeking. Have you tried the Sacred Groves? She may be working on the shrines today or participating in rituals.'

I looked up at him, hopefully. 'No. Where are these groves?'

'In the rainforest on the edge of the town. I can accompany you if you wish.'

Ebis turned to me and nodded. It was worth a try. We all piled into the car.

'My name is Femi', the young man said, extending his hand and gripping ours tightly in return.

'And what will we discover there, Femi?' asked Ebis.

Femi grinned. 'You will be sure to discover gods there. It is their home.'

I felt a rush of excitement. 'And will we find her there too?'

'Maybe,' he sighed 'but she may not wish to speak with you. She does not always welcome tourists.'

'Well *I'm* certainly no tourist' I was unaware how arrogant I sounded until I realised the two guys were laughing at me.

A strange mood descended as we entered the Sacred Groves. Apart from the rustling of leaves and birdsong, silence reigned. I sensed I was being propelled into another world; an intense, primeval world, yet, simultaneously, a world that was light and benign. The further we strolled through the groves the more enchanted I became.

Some of the sculptures dotted amongst the trees were human in both shape and scale, others, in clearings, were the opposite: as tall as trees — bizarre, oblong shapes in wood, cement and metal, sprouting unfamiliar limbs which stretched up to the sky. Unlike anything I'd ever seen before, their sheer artistry and preternatural beauty mesmerised and intrigued me. I looked around. I could certainly sense a presence — or presences.

What are these sculptures all about, Femi?

'They are shrines of the *orisha* – the gods and goddesses of Ifa.'

'And what *is* Ifa, exactly?'

'In a nutshell, it is the 7,000-year-old religion of the Yoruba peoples.'

'Did it originate here?'

'Not here, but in the ancient Yoruba kingdom of Ilé-Ifè nearby.'

We came to an opening beside a river. A Yoruba woman dressed in a white robe was sitting on the river bank cracking open a pile of kola nuts.

'Is that her?' I asked, breathlessly.

'No, that is not her,' Femi replied. He wandered over to the woman and said something in Yoruba. She shook her head.

He turned to me. 'She has not come to the Groves today.'

'Please ask where she might be.'

They conferred again. The woman simply laughed and shrugged her shoulders.

'It is possible she is travelling,' Femi suggested.

'So who was that woman in white, if it wasn't her?' I whispered, as we walked away.

'She is the priestess who guards the shrine over there.' He pointed to a Gaudiesque, cave-like structure which I would later discover symbolised both a womb and the gate to eternity.

'Can I go inside it, Femi?'

'Yes, but the madam will expect you to place in her hand some recompense for protecting and cleaning the sacred space.'

Ebis rattled around with the change in his pockets. I walked over and handed the woman a five *naire* note.

At first glance the inside of 'the cave' was something of a disappointment. Devoid of the relics, ornaments or candles I'd somehow been expecting, it appeared to be nothing more than a dusty, empty shell. Then, all of a sudden, I felt suffocatingly hot, sweaty and grimy. My pulse started racing and I began to hyperventilate. Instead of sitting down, I ran, on an impulse, to the river bank, where I knelt down and plunged my face, head, chest, arms and hands in the clear river water.

I was unaware, at the time, that this river was the Oshun River – the birthplace of the river goddess herself – or that it was her shrine I'd just entered. But what I do remember, after bathing my upper body in the water, is being taken over by a powerful feeling of connectedness to everything around me; a kind of euphoric love-fest, the like of which I'd never known.

'Your eyes are shining,' Ebis remarked, as I dried my face on my T-shirt.

'Perhaps she has been touched by the goddess,' Femi laughed.

'Who or what exactly, is this goddess?' I was bursting with curiosity. We sat beside the shrine and Femi explained that Oshun was one of the sixteen primary *orisha*. So important was she that the Nigerian state we were in had been named after her, too.

Femi looked at me. 'Oshun is a particular favourite with women. She also goes by the name of Mammy Water.'

I plied him with question upon question until he glanced at his watch and abruptly stood up.

'She has the answers to your questions. You will need to return to her house in Ibokun Road. Please, I must leave now to meet my fiancée from work.'

'We can drop you off,' Ebis offered. 'Where does she work?'

'Back in town; in the offices of an indigo warehouse.'

'And you? Femi, what is your occupation?'

His smile faded. 'I am training to be an engineer but my studies at Ibadan University have been halted because the lecturers have not been paid for seven months.'

We commiserated with Femi as we drove back into the town, and shared our concerns about the sorry state of the country and the appalling level of corruption in government.

After dropping Femi off, Ebis and I returned to the house in Ibokun Road. I knocked on the door, more gently this time, but there was still no response.

'Perhaps you are not yet ready,' said Ebis, with a knowing laugh; the kind of laugh Africans come out with when they've grasped the deeper reality behind an impasse such as this one, which westerners, like myself, so often take at face value.

High Priestess

MY CURIOSITY in this Oshogbo woman had been aroused the week before. I was sipping warm beer on my friend Boye's sweltering, candlelit balcony – courtesy of yet another Lagos blackout – when his eyes suddenly flashed with excitement.

'There is someone you should check out while you are still in the country, Diane.'

'Oh yes?'

'A high priestess of the goddess Oshun, no less. She lives in the town of Oshogbo. Virtually single-handedly, she has been battling fundamentalist Christians and Muslims, and has managed to bring about a revival of the Yoruba faith of Ifa. Her power, it is said, is formidable.'

I was surprised to hear this from Boye – Dr Bamgboye Afolabi, to give him his correct title – as he was the leader of the Nigerian branch of the Buddhist organisation I belong to.

'How did you hear about her?'

'My mum is the *Aare Iyalode* of Oshogbo – the second-in-command to the head of all the women in Oshogboland.'

'Wow! I'd like to meet your mum and this priestess.'

'They say she is also an artist.'

'Her name is…?'

'Adunni Olorisha.'

Ten days after our visit to Oshogbo, Ebis called me from Abuja where he'd just been posted on a three-month-long secondment. To save me another possibly fruitless trip he'd offered to make the journey to Abuja via Oshogbo and attempt to interview the high priestess on my behalf.

'I met with her…very powerful,' he murmured, with an unfamiliar note of sternness in his voice. The phone line was dreadful. The only other words I could make out were 'frightened' and 'witch' before the line went dead, as it so often did in Nigeria.

Ebis frightened? I was perplexed. I had him down as someone with masses of courage. A few days before he left for Abuja we'd been escorted out of a restaurant where we were having lunch as one of 'the big boys' – as Ebis called the businessmen and politicians whose corrupt practices he exposed on his radio show – had demanded his removal. Ebis claimed this happened quite frequently. I suspected the Abuja secondment was for his personal safety.

I also recalled how unusually quiet the normally ebullient Ebis had been in the Sacred Groves, and wondered if this had something to do with his upbringing. For Nigerian Christians, all traditional religions were taboo, and often denounced as witchcraft or devil worship. His call both piqued my curiosity and left me wondering what I might be letting myself in for.

A few days later, I headed, once again, for Oshogbo – this time alone. The drive down in a rattling old VW Beetle was even slower and hotter than the previous one. By the time the driver pulled into Oshogbo, anxiety was flooding through me at the prospect of both meeting – and of not meeting – this High Priestess.

I knocked politely on the door; this time it opened. A Yoruba woman of middle-age, her hair in braids and holding a besom-like broom stood in the doorway and stared at me with silent suspicion.

'Adunni?' I asked, believing this to be her.

'Who are you?' she demanded, accusingly. I gave her my name and a few brief details.

'Wait!' she commanded, closing the door in my face. She returned a minute or two later and motioned to me to come inside.

I followed her up some steps to a large, dark studio filled with canvases, carvings and melted candles. Weathered-looking books lined a couple of shelves. Strange drawings and scribbles covered the faded-blue walls. The woman who had let me in nodded in the direction of a slender, behatted figure, dressed in black, who had her back to me and was staring out of the window. Turning slowly, she walked towards me, extending her hand. Her hair was dyed black and black eye-liner encircled her eyes, but her skin, I noticed, was white.

As a young teenager I'd feasted on the novels of Rider H Haggard – until I grew a little more world-savvy and found his racial slurs and imperialist agenda irritating – and here I was, confronted by a formidable, white, *She*-like high priestess in the depths of Africa. This one clearly hadn't bathed in the flame of life, which promised eternal youth, like Haggard's Ayesha, but she still stirred something in the depths of my imagination. And I sensed I was, without doubt, in the presence of another *She who must be obeyed*.

Getting to know the high priestess wasn't easy. She was never one for small talk.

'I'm not quite sure how I should address you. What does Adunni Olorisha mean, exactly?'

'Beloved of the gods.'

'Should I call you that?'

'Adunni is fine. Please, be seated.' She pulled out a three-legged stool from under a bench but remained standing herself.

'Your accent, Adunni, it sounds German.'

'I was born in Austria. Why are you here?'

'I…I think I experienced the power of Oshun in the Sacred Groves when I splashed my face in the river… A surge of energy – like an electric current – flowed through me, along with a feeling…' I paused to allow my embarrassment to surface '…of love for everyone and everything… It left me wanting to know more about Oshun and the *orisha*…and you and your work, Adunni.'

She turned away and yawned. She'd heard it all before; many times.

'I'd really like to write about your work in the Groves and I think a documentary might…'

'And why are you here *in Nigeria*?' she interrupted, impatiently.

I explained how, after my divorce, my young son Sacha's Colombian father, Roberto, who was the partner in a French-Colombian architectural practice, had moved out to Lagos to open an Africa office. So that Sacha could continue to see his father, we agreed that Roberto would pay for our flights and Sacha and I would spend his school holidays out there.

'Your son is on holiday in November? That is unusual.'

'No. This time I'm here without him because I'm about to start rehearsals for a play I've written called *Victoria Island*.'

'And what is this play of yours about?' She looked remotely interested for the first time.

'After a few trips out here the grimmer aspects of Nigeria started to get under my skin...'

'*Grimmer* aspects?'

'...The widespread corruption; the armed robbery; public executions on Lagos' Bar Beach...the girls pressured by poverty into becoming sex workers in dives like Club 21...the behaviour of many British and European contractors, along with their workers and their wives who came over with the oil boom...'

'Why did you call this play *Victoria Island*?'

'Because Victoria Island is where many of the expats and the wealthy Nigerians in Lagos live...'

'I know Victoria Island.'

'...Well, its bland modern buildings and leafy avenues provide the perfect setting for the play. Some of the expats living there and in Ikoyi behave like they're Lord and Lady of the Manor. They treat their stewards like dirt...'

'Victoria Island is a swamp,' she remarked. 'The British colonial government created its landmass on swampland beside the Atlantic Ocean to halt the breeding of mosquitoes.'

'I...I didn't know that...but it intrigued me,' I continued, 'how quickly people can change when given the chance to lord it over others, and how some can cave in so easily to the lures of money and illicit sex.'

'And so you decided to write a play about it.' She pulled up a chair and sat down.

'Yes, but I didn't expect to be acting in it myself.'

'So why *are* you acting in it yourself?'

Only then did it dawn on me that *she* was interviewing *me*. I knew, instinctively, that she wanted to ascertain whether I was a worthy enough subject upon whom to expend her precious time.

Nervously, I went on to explain how not one of the few white actors living out there would agree to perform in either of the two white roles. 'Strong meat for this part of the world' was how one posh actor had described the script.

'Three actors have already been cast for each of the four Nigerian roles,' I told her, 'but once they, the director and the stage crew have been paid, the theatre doesn't have enough money left to bring actors over from England – or even to properly pay me.'

'Job sharing amongst Africans is common. It is one of the ways they look after one another. Despite the oil wealth enjoyed by one per cent of the country, very little of it trickles down to the ninety-nine per cent below.'

'I agree with that in principle,' I replied, 'but it puts up costs. I've trained as an actress and the only way the play is going to happen is if I perform in it myself. Fortunately, my brother, Neil, who has had a little acting experience, has agreed to play the white male role.'

I didn't mention that I had no work lined up in London once the run had finished. And that was why I was there. Tentatively, I raised the subject of a documentary proposal again. She stood up and walked over to the window.

'What you experienced by the river that day was nothing! Nothing!' She sighed. 'During the Oshun festival the crowds become wild on Oshun energy. Even the horses are possessed.'

'I'm sure that would provide great footage…'

'If you really want to know this *orisha*'s power it is necessary to engage in rituals.'

She registered my involuntary shudder.

'I've heard that animal sacrifices take place during these rituals… I'd find that difficult, I'm afraid… I'm a vegetarian, you see.'

'So am I,' she replied, 'but you have to understand that the shedding of blood is a symbolic shattering of the boundary that exists between human and *orisha*. The sacrifice enables us to connect on the same plane. The animals themselves consider it an honour to spill their blood for a god or goddess.'

'Mmmm… I've been known to faint at the sight of blood – animal and human.'

She shook her head. 'Europeans are a barrel of neuroses and complexes, aren't they, my dear?'

I nodded – feeling very small. She could see into me. As much as I admired Adunni and her work, if the truth be known, Ebis wasn't the only one. I was more than just a little in awe of her. I was scared shitless.

She continued to stare out of the window for what felt like an age. I knew she was making up her mind. Finally she turned to face me.

'To have written this play of yours you must be a woman of some courage, but still you are fearful and doubt yourself. You have had a taste of the energy of Oshun and she could be a source of strength to you, if you allow her. Leave me now. I have work to do. But you may return to visit when your play is over.'

Fear pestered me throughout the rehearsal period of the play and into the run itself. I didn't, at that time, know enough about the workings of Oshun to avail myself of her supportive energies.

Before we moved into the theatre, rehearsals took place on the stage of an outdoor arena in the searing heat of downtown Surulere. I was rodent-phobic, and seeing rats the size of cats creep along the arena walls freaked me out. I fought a few confidence-shredding battles with the director, Sam, who was also a well-known TV actor with ego and alcohol issues. And the opening night itself was very nearly a disaster.

For most occasions of any significance in Nigeria, an official opening ceremony is demanded – which usually involves a very long, very formal speech by a local worthy. The person invited by the director to perform this duty was a bigwig, *alhaji* chief whom I hadn't even met. He kept the cast and audience waiting for an hour before phoning the theatre to say there had been a flood and that he couldn't make it as the road was full of potholes. The audience was growing restless. In desperation, the director cast his eye around the auditorium and noticed an imposing-looking gentleman who had stood up to remove his jacket and was folding it over the back of his chair. On an impulse, Sam went over to this stranger and asked him if he would introduce the play. By fortuitous coincidence the gentleman in question was Boye, my Buddhist doctor friend, whom I'd invited to the first night along with his wife, Akua.

During the run itself I had to learn to relinquish control and be prepared for the totally unexpected. By British standards the play would have been X-rated, so I was shocked one afternoon when I came on stage for a matinee performance to see that the auditorium was full of schoolkids. Based on a satirical one-liner, *you should not smoke that nasty stuff*, directed at a character smoking weed, the headmaster, believing the play, which he'd seen the night before, carried a virulent anti-drugs message, had herded along the entire school. The kids found every scene hilariously funny.

Another time I walked into the dressing room and discovered the three Nigerian actresses who had each been allocated the lead female role physically fighting each other over whose turn it was to go on stage that evening; a nightmare to have to sort out just before a performance.

Overall, the production was a rewarding, fun experience though, and I learned a great deal. Even a row which flared up between myself and my usually passive brother somehow enabled him to get truly under the skin of the character he was playing and resulted in a brilliant, final performance. In retrospect, though, I came to understand why the British Council wanted to stick with the likes of Shakespeare and Dickens as cultural exports, and even why priggish white actors hadn't wanted to be associated with the play; it hit a few too many raw nerves.

By the end of the run I'd spent long enough immersed in the less savoury, political and social side of Nigerian life and I was more than ready to begin exploring the spiritual.

River Goddess

I DIDN'T see Adunni again until the following Easter. Once the play was over I was missing my son so much I flew straight home. I wrote to her, via the Austrian Embassy in Lagos, apologising for not visiting her before I left. I didn't receive a reply.

Back in London, between the odd bits of writing and performing work that came my way, I spent my time in the library at the School of Oriental and African Studies in Bloomsbury, reading up about the *orisha* – and in particular, Oshun.

I learned that for the Yoruba, love equates with harmony and Oshun, the river goddess, is seen as the force of harmony. She is 'the unseen mother present at every gathering' who has been allocated the task of granting children. Embodying all aspects of womanhood, the goddess enjoys bathing herself, loves gold and carries around a mirror to admire her beauty and sensuality. Apart from the habit of going about her daily business with a pot of honey hanging around her waist – so far so normal.

Yet I was struck by how much she also presents a refreshing

perspective on womanhood – one that has little in common with the patriarchal mindset so firmly embedded in western culture. Proud of her sexuality, Oshun feels no shame, is her own fiercely independent woman – or rather goddess – refusing to kowtow to the demands of her husband or her children. She sacrifices neither herself nor her creativity to the will of others, and becomes angry not through jealousy but through injustice. There is nothing subservient about this goddess.

Over thousands of years, umpteen female deities in assorted shapes and sizes have been worshipped in countless cultures the world over. Traditional favourites such as the Roman goddess Diana and the Egyptian goddess Isis are still revered today, along with a panoply of others – from the Aborigine Holy Goddess Mumuna the Great-Mother-Who-Made-Us-All, to the Great Mother in Europe and Amaterasu No Kami, the Japanese Goddess of the Sun. Their countries of origin may be diverse, but the deities themselves and the form their worship takes have much in common; the goddess cult appears both universal and inclusive – neither culture nor colour are a barrier to worshipping the female deity of your choice.

But the goddess who had drawn me in was Oshun. And in her it was possible to see another type of womanhood; one that I aspired to – a fearless, empowered womanhood. Oludomare, Ifa's chief divinity, so admired Oshun's feisty, assertive behaviour that he issued an oracle with a salutary, feminist message:

> *The person who is not well-learned is the person who will say a woman does not amount to anything in life. Let no-one use negative language on women… We are all born by women… Let us kneel and prostrate before women.* (Odu Ose Otura)

When I finally managed to locate Adunni on my next visit to Oshogbo she was perched on a ladder in the Sacred Groves. The ladder itself was propped precariously on bamboo scaffolding that encircled the shrine she was working on. I was intrigued that Adunni and the monkeys jumping on and off the scaffolding clearly knew one another. I'd been expecting a frosty reception but she smiled down at me, nodded, and simply carried on working. I sat myself on the dry grass at the foot of the shrine and took out a flask and two beakers.

'Would you like a Chapman, Adunni? It's the non-alcoholic version. My ex's steward prepared it in Lagos. It's still very cold.'

'No thank-you. I have water here.'

'Isn't it a bit unnerving,' I ventured, after a few minutes of silence, 'working on scaffolding made of bamboo? I didn't know it existed.'

'Bamboo is much tougher than it looks or feels,' she bellowed down at me, trying to be heard over the racket the monkeys were making. 'Much like you – and women in general.'

'I did some reading up on these female *orisha* when I was in London. Pretty powerful, aren't they?'

'Yes. Yoruba women used to be powerful, too.' Dipping her hand into her pocket, she took out a few nuts and fed them to a monkey that was hanging by one arm from the scaffolding above. 'Not only did they rule the marketplace, they were also the owners of property and land – which they passed on to their daughters or nieces when they died. They had a say over the appointment of kings and matters of justice.'

'So what happened?' I asked, getting to my feet.

'What happened?' She slowly descended the ladder. 'Colonialism happened. Colonisers invoked European land reforms to transfer land from women to men and appointed tame kings to do their bidding.'

She knelt down, spread a piece of cloth on the grass and proceeded to wrap up her tools. Then she rinsed her hands with water from a plastic bottle, and opened out a tatty, black umbrella.

'Didn't the women object?'

'Of course they objected! But the male rulers, black and white, were committed to destroying women's power – political, economic and spiritual.'

'Nothing new there.' I was surprised at the strength of the anger I felt on behalf of these women who had been so brutally divested of their rights.

'Come, let us walk a little.' Adunni steered me along a well-worn path under the shade of her umbrella.

'Women also lost control of the *orisha* shrines and places of worship they had previously owned, like this one.' She stopped in her tracks, sighed, and gesticulated around the Groves. 'Ceremonies and initiations traditionally conducted by women were taken over by men, who wore masks and dresses in order to appease the *orisha*.'

I giggled. 'I bet the goddesses weren't fooled.'

'Of course they were not fooled. It was a pathetic attempt to usurp female power. But this disbarring of women from the shrines, along with *orisha* worshippers being denied an education and work opportunities unless they converted to Christianity, led to Ifa's near-obliteration. They didn't have the money to repair old shrines or to construct new ones – which resulted in their decay.'

Wrinkling her nose, Adunni bent down to pick up a cigarette butt. 'And we're still clearing up the mess.'

We walked together in silence until she stopped abruptly in her tracks, looking momentarily concerned.

'Are you a Christian, Diane?'

'I'm a Buddhist.'

'Ah…I was once very interested in Buddhism,' she smiled, 'especially the Tibetan variety. It has much in common with Ifa; the interconnectedness of the physical and the metaphysical.'

'The Buddhism I practise, based on the Lotus Sutra, also has a feminist agenda: women possess Buddhahood, too. Other sutras claim we must create sufficiently good karma to be born a man before we can even start thinking about the possibility of enlightenment…'

To my surprise she gently grasped my elbow and guided me to a path which led down to the river. We emerged into the clearing between Oshun's shrine and the water. I was back, once again, in the spot where I'd had my first taste of the goddess. Adunni squatted down at the entrance to the shrine and motioned to me to sit beside her. She proceeded to launch into what felt like an impromptu lecture on world religions in general; how, I imagined, a wise old tribal elder would address an eager young neophyte. After a while she got to her feet and strolled down to the river.

'More people should know the truth of *orisha*,' she murmured, as if thinking aloud. 'These gods belong to everyone.'

She turned and looked at me. '…Providing what you write is neither sensationalist nor exclusively about me, and the *orisha* – Oshun in particular – is featured and respectfully portrayed, then you may go ahead with this proposal.'

Tears of relief welled up in my eyes. 'Of course, Adunni. I promise.'

'When time permits, I am prepared to cooperate with you.'

Artist

DUSK IN the Sacred Groves. The crickets were making such a racket we could hardly hear one another speak. Adunni paused to watch one of her small team of artists repair the sculptural fence around a damaged shrine. With rusty-looking nails stashed between his teeth and red dust clinging to his sweaty torso, he hammered away, oblivious to the heat, the mosquitoes and even to our presence.

Adunni raised her voice. 'Art belongs in the open. Its function is primarily spiritual – to encapsulate the wonder and mystery of nature and our universe.' She bent down and picked up the young man's tools and rearranged them in a neat pile. He smiled at her and nodded.

'But you used to exhibit in galleries, didn't you? I read somewhere that you founded the Art Club in Vienna.'

'Along with a couple of other artists, yes.'

'And before that you attended the Vienna Academy of Fine Art?' She nodded.

'Wasn't that the academy that rejected Hitler?'

'Yes,' she grimaced. 'Twice.'

'I read somewhere it was his hatred of the Jewish professor who rejected him that triggered his anti-Semitism?'

She shrugged her shoulders. She didn't want to talk about it.

Adunni was much happier when discussing Ifa, the *orisha* and art than she was her personal life. But by now I'd managed to find out that she was born in Graz, Austria, in 1915, the daughter of Swiss/German parents, and that her birth name was Suzanne Wenger. I'd also discovered that as an artist she'd exhibited widely in Europe. In Paris she'd held exhibitions at the Galerie Faubourg, St Honoré, the Galerie Creuze in the Huitième Quartier, and Galerie Lambert on the Rive Gauche. But I was keen to know much more. What had her life been like in Europe? Why had she come to Nigeria? Mindful of not wishing to jeopardise our fledgling relationship by appearing too prying, I kept hoping she'd volunteer the information herself. That evening she was more forthcoming than usual.

'Not long after we established the Arts Club I won some money in an Italian poster competition, so I went to Switzerland in search of other modern artists. Someone directed me to the Galerie Des Eaux Vives in Zurich, where I met Hansegger. He founded the Abstrakt-Konkret group.'

'Abstrakt-Konkret? I haven't heard of it.'

'The group included Klee, Mondrian, Arp, Tauber and others. I was much younger than most of them. Hansegger bought my entire portfolio on the condition that he could pay me in Paris. He had more money there. He also wanted to get me out of Vienna. The conservatism of the place was stifling me.'

'Wasn't that where you met Ulli Beier?'

She gave me a sidelong glance. 'I see you have been doing your research.'

I had indeed. Suzanne was already an established artist living in Paris when she met the long-haired linguist and ethnologist Ulli Beier. A few years her junior, Beier was working in London as a teacher at the time. The Nazis had shut down his father's Berlin medical practice in 1933, and he, along with the rest of his German-Jewish family, had moved to Palestine. During the war, Beier was interned by the British authorities as an enemy alien. Despite this affront, he decided, once the war was over, to move to England and study linguistics at London University.

'Ulli was on holiday in Paris when I met him,' Adunni volunteered.

'And so what brought you to Nigeria?'

'Destiny.'

Ulli had only just fallen in love with Suzanne when he spotted an advertisement for a position as lecturer in English at University College, Ibadan, in the west of Nigeria. He was offered the post on one condition: that he was married. The possibility of a lonely, white bachelor shacking up with a nubile young African was presumably something the colonial authorities were anxious to avoid.

Culture-curious Suzanne agreed to come along for the ride. Beier shared her bohemian take on life, and contempt for empty social rituals. The registrar reprimanded them for making a joke out of the sacred institution of marriage when they turned up at the registry office with an assortment of curtain rings.

Nigeria is now an independent nation with the largest economy in Africa, but when Suzanne arrived in 1950 it was still under British rule. Empire-builders in the previous century had forced together 250 ethnic and linguistic groups with multiple different belief systems under one colonial umbrella.

'Do you know how this country received its illustrious name?' Adunni's tone was sarcastic. I did, actually. But perhaps, because of my nationality, she was determined to tell me anyway.

'Flora Shaw, the English wife of the Governor-General, Lord Frederick Lugard, performed the arduous task of joining together the Latin adjective *niger*, meaning black, with the noun *area*. What a paucity of imagination to bestow so puerile a label on such a culturally rich, diverse people!'

We were getting sidetracked. I wanted to get the conversation back onto her. 'Wasn't it difficult, to begin with, leaving behind the European art scene?'

'Not in the slightest. I immersed myself in learning an ancient form of cassava batik-making known as *adire*. I still make them occasionally. We use starch from the cassava plant and indigo dye to depict scenes from Yoruba myths. Would you care to see some..?'

'I'd love to.' We began making our way back.

'After a time,' she said, half to herself, 'I began to find the idea of exhibiting in galleries strange and even a bit sick.'

'Why, Adunni?'

'Repairing these shrines and building new ones involved working outdoors. My art became living art; spiritual art; not dead canvas stuck to sterile walls.'

We stopped briefly at the Odi shrine. 'As you can see, I had connected with the powerful, primordial divinities which reside here in the Groves; they communicated artistic visions to me.'

The Odi was a breathtaking complex mass of egg-like shapes and tentacles which she was still in the process of creating. Odi means deaf and dumb – that which is beyond our comprehension.

Scenes from the *Alien* films flashed through my mind. The shrine reminded me of the artist HR Giger's *Alien* creations. I stared in wonder; the Odi emanated an energy; an unnervingly 'live' energy. She looked it over with pride.

When we entered her scruffy little shop on the ground floor

of her house in Oshogbo, I couldn't help thinking how it was worlds apart from those galleries on the Left Bank she'd once exhibited in. Adunni proudly showed off a few of the batiks her artists had produced, and some of her own. They struck me as more intricate and intensely colourful than any batik I'd previously seen. I regret, to this day, not buying one.

Gin & Drums

MARRIAGE brought Suzanne to Nigeria; over thirty years later, divorce brought me. Suzanne's Nigeria was still a colonial one and mine in the early stages of independence, but each held a different set of challenges.

The Nigerian writer and Nobel laureate, Wole Soyinka, described Ulli and Suzanne's happenstance in his country as: *an assignment roulette in Europe that brought them to Nigeria.* Once there, according to Soyinka, *both promptly 'went native', Suzanne not just culturally, but viscerally and spiritually, holding nothing back in herself.* As for me, I didn't *go native.* I lost a sense of who I was entirely.

'You don't like whisky?' Adunni asked me one humid evening as we sat outside on her terrace. She'd noticed that I'd hardly touched a drop of the scotch I'd bought for her. Someone had given me the nod it was her favourite tipple.

'Goes straight to my head,' I said, apologetically. 'Don't know why. I'm OK with vodka and gin – now and then.'

'Ah! Gin!' she responded, wrinkling her nose. 'I grew so tired of gin and tonic, gin and tonic, gin and tonic – that was all they ever drank in the university compound. The wives of these academics claimed it was because of the quinine in the tonic – which was rubbish. I drank a lot of it too, but as a cure for boredom. Lemon grass is a more effective anti-malarial.'

When they first arrived in Nigeria, Suzanne and Ulli were housed in the university compound in Ibadan, which was peopled mainly by Brits who kept themselves to themselves and had little interest in the indigenous people or their culture. Such segregation was anathema to Suzanne.

'Was it a culture shock coming here all those years ago?'

'Culture shock? I didn't get to see any culture for a long while – except English culture. The conversations were so tedious. Mainly college gossip or what was happening back in England.'

She attempted to mimic an upper-class English accent. '"You are an artist, are you? Oh, how very interesting. Do you play bridge?" It was a relief,' she grimaced, 'when I caught tuberculosis.'

Early on, I too had had an unsavoury run-in with gin and tonic. When our plane landed in Lagos, on our first ever visit, my son and I were refused permission to enter the country and ordered to take the next flight home. It had taken weeks of queuing and battling red tape at the Nigerian Consulate in London to obtain our visas in the first place. The curmudgeonly approach adopted by consulate employees to the granting of visas was heralded as payback time for the Brits. According to the immigration officer at Murtala Mohammed airport we had to be deported because I'd only allowed ten days to elapse following our yellow fever inoculations instead of the regulation fourteen. The issue was eventually resolved, however, by my ex-husband, Roberto, giving an enormous 'dash' to an airport 'fixer' who surreptitiously handed a smaller 'dash' to the immigration officer concerned. The 'dash' being a legacy of the Brits who would press a *naire* into a Nigerian's palm and say something along the lines of: 'Dash over to mess, Boy, and collect my khakis.'

On my first evening in Nigeria, to recover from that stressful threat of imminent deportation, I sat on the balcony of my ex-husband's elegant house in the upmarket Lagos district of Ikoyi, quaffing vast quantities of gin and tonic. So busy was I admiring the coconut-laden palm trees, clusters of amaryllis, frangipani and African lilies that his gardener was watering in the lush, tropical garden that I forgot all about insect repellent. I awoke the next morning with a crashing hangover, itching all over. My feet, in particular, had been so badly bitten by mosquitoes they'd swollen to twice their size. I had a temperature, and fretting about the possibility of cerebral malaria or dengue fever, Roberto rushed off to the French Embassy and came back with a young doctor called Pierre, who injected me in the groin with some noxious substance and gave me a bucket-load of meds to swallow; a most inauspicious beginning. I couldn't touch gin for years after that.

'My life here only began in earnest,' Adunni continued, 'once we moved out of the university compound to the town of Ede.' She stood up to light a couple of candles. 'Ulli became increasingly involved in documenting every aspect he could of Yoruba culture. The oral history, drama, literature and poetry of the Yoruba fascinated him.'

'And you, Adunni, what fascinated you?' She leaned over and filled her cracked beaker with whisky.

'The drumming – its spiritual aspect. That is what fascinated me.'

She went on to describe how, on her fourth evening in Ede, she was lured into the forest by the sound of drumming. And it was here that she first encountered a disappearing generation of Yoruba priests and priestesses who were engaged in *orisha* rituals. She was mesmerised. They, in turn, identified in her the same level of clairvoyance and an 'archaic consciousness' that they themselves possessed. She was welcomed as one of their own. An aged, blind priest called Aajagemo predicted that in the future she would build *petesi* – homes of more than one storey – for the gods. After her encounter with the Ede priests and priestesses Suzanne underwent something of a spiritual metamorphosis.

The 'culture' that I first encountered in Nigeria involved drumming, too. It was anything but spiritual.

Pierre, the French doctor, had invited Roberto and me to the thirtieth birthday party of a colleague who also worked at the French Embassy. The plan was to go on from the party to watch the musician and controversial political activist, Fela Kuti, perform at The Shrine – his bespoke venue in the Lagos suburb of Ikedja.

We were late getting to the party. Although plenty of wine and beer were left, all the food had disappeared, apart from the large, half-eaten birthday cake, which, I was surprised to learn, was a banana cake. It looked and tasted more like a chocolate cake. Not wanting to drink on an empty stomach, I scoffed a load of it. Then a small group of us piled into the embassy minibus and headed for The Shrine.

Onstage, at the open-air, corrugated-iron-roofed stadium,

Fela was strutting around in a white, Elvis-in-Vegas-type suit, to the deafening thud of Afro-beat music. Suspended above him, in gigantic birdcages were his 'wives' – skimpily-clad women dancing maniacally; their cages swinging from side to side.

I looked around. We were the only Europeans present. There were hundreds of Nigerian guys wandering around the stadium, but I couldn't see any women – apart from Sylvie, a French-Moroccan embassy employee, myself and the caged ladies. My head started to spin. I suddenly felt faint. Pierre found me a chair and crouched down beside me.

''Ow much cake you eat?' he asked.

'Two or three pieces...I was starving. Now I feel sick.'

'Ah, but ze 'ashish 'ere very strong.'

'Hashish? They told me it was banana cake!'

Pierre broke into paroxysms of laughter. '*Abana* cake! Nigeria name for 'ashish. One *petit morceau* enough to get you 'igh.'

'Shit!'

He then proceeded to share the joke with the others, who began pointing at me and doubling up with what I now realised was stoned laughter. As if the situation couldn't get any worse, Fela, dripping with sweat, abruptly stopped the music, and asked for a minute's silence to pay homage to the ancestors and the gods. Then he launched into a rabid anti-Britain, anti-Thatcher diatribe. It was still the era of apartheid, and boy, did he loathe Maggie. A few years later, on the cover of his album, *Beasts of No Nation*, he depicts her with horns and fangs dripping with blood. In my *abana*-induced, paranoid head-state, I was convinced Fela's rant was directed at me, and that the crowd were glaring at our tiny group of privileged white faces.

In what I assumed to be a generous gesture of reconciliation, a young Nigerian guy with a lovely smile approached me, extended his hand, and asked me to dance. A sea of black faces searched for my response. I was desperate to dance with him – to cement this gesture of friendship; to display unity. I wanted everyone to know that I, too, hated Thatcher's policies and British imperialism. But I couldn't stand up. My legs, quite literally, were refusing to support the rest of my body. The paranoia intensified; they could interpret this as a hostile response on my part; I needed to escape as soon as possible.

I called out to Roberto to take me home. Once outside, for the first and the last time in my adult life, I wet myself.

I was only in my early twenties when I first arrived in Nigeria, and Suzanne ten years older, but I, nevertheless, considered my initial responses to this unfamiliar land and its people pathetic compared to hers. I envied her fearless curiosity and defiant attitude towards the establishment; her Oshun-like courage. As time passed I craved to be more like her.

Orisha

THE HEAT was fierce. I'd been trailing behind Adunni in the Groves for what felt like hours. Hot and thirsty, I'd drunk all my water. Twice my age, she showed no signs of faltering, or of thirst.

'You don't drink much of this,' I remarked, waving my empty water bottle at her.

She shook her head. 'Water is a precious commodity here, to be respected...'

'Of course it is...the droughts...'

'...There is a well-known Yoruba proverb: *no one is an enemy to water.*'

It was impossible to make a passing comment without Adunni delivering some gnomic response or other. I made a note to myself to think twice before blurting out trivia.

She came to a halt at last, beneath the hand-carved shrine of Iya Moopo, the 'Great Mother' goddess of indigo – an abstract, tentacled structure 10 metres high and 25 metres long. She'd designed the Iya Moopo herself, and constructed it with the aid of her team of craftsmen – a couple of whom were leaning against the shrine, eating their lunch. They chatted with Adunni in Yoruba.

Not long after she and Ulli moved from Ede to Oshogbo, Adunni began assembling a group of Yoruba artists and craftsmen and women to help her in the mammoth task of repairing and constructing shrines in the Sacred Groves. With the *orisha* as their muse, the group believed in 'art as ritual', and called themselves The New Sacred Artists.

'I find it humbling, standing here, looking up at this,' I sighed. 'The workmanship is phenomenal.'

Adunni stroked the Iya Moopo as you would a cat. 'Each *orisha* represents a different aspect of the human psyche, or the universe, looked at from a different angle, you know.'

'That's fascinating. I read somewhere that the *orisha* are akin to Jungian archetypes – although I'm not really sure what Jungian archetypes are, exactly.'

'Ha! Jung! That is what educated westerners like to believe,' she replied, 'but it irks me. It is patronising. You could also say that Jungian thinking has much in common with Ifa, which came first.'

'And they've also been compared to Greek gods?'

'Yes, but that is a mistake, too. Ifa's gods are far more multifarious and complex than those within the Greek pantheon. There are 401 variations of the 16 primary *orisha*. Their anthropomorphic forms represent powerful and dissonant universal energies…'

'401! Do you know them all?'

'Of course I know them all. Shall I explain some of them to you?'

'Please.'

Although I tried my best to hide it, with the exception of

Oshun, I was, at that time, more interested in Adunni and her work than in her plethora of complicated gods. I still had a pile of questions I was dying to ask about her life, but to keep her on board I knew I needed to go along with her sometimes convoluted *orisha* explanations. That day, however, my curiosity about these forces of nature was shortly to be aroused.

'What do you mean by *dissonant* universal energies, Adunni?'

'Well, much like human beings, the *orisha* are a bag of contradictions. Take Shango for example...'

'Isn't he the god of thunder, lightning and war?'

'Yes...but before he became an *orisha*, Shango was said to be a powerful, violent ruler, who reigned for seven years, during which time he relentlessly killed and maimed his own people. One legend has it that while experimenting with gunpowder he blew up his palace, killing his three wives and all of his children...'

'And yet he still became a god?'

'The *orisha* are not icons of purity and perfection which humans would struggle to live up to, or could only identify with at the expense of repressing our lower nature.'

'What about Shango's wives?'

'In his *orisha* incarnation, Shango is married to Oshun...'

'But isn't that the same as the union between Venus and Mars; the goddess of love and the god of war in classical mythology?'

'Not quite. Shango is also married to another powerful female, Oya, the *orisha* of wind, violent storms, chaotic upheaval and sudden change.'

'So tranquil Oshun and tempestuous Oya are love rivals, then?'

'But Ifa plays around with gender stereotypes. This cyclonic goddess is sometimes portrayed with a beard.'

'Why a beard?'

'Oya is a warrior, too. She often fights alongside her husband.

In pre-colonial times gender roles in Africa were fluid. Men could be 'mothers'; and women, 'sons' and 'husbands'. 'Male' daughters were able to lead the tribe.'

'You don't see many female heads of state in Africa now, do you?'

'Colonial power structures changed all that.' Adunni looked up at the still, cloudless sky as if willing Oya to make an appearance, but the goddess was clearly having a day off.

'Oya's tornado-like aggressive spirit is known to trigger undesirable vicissitudes in life. Contrary to popular thinking in western cultures, females also possess some of the less appealing, violent qualities traditionally associated with males...'

I nodded in agreement.

'...and we are capable of doing the same work...Oya is also in charge of the marketplace. She controls business, and is responsible for sudden swings in the financial markets and stable currencies plummeting. There are bankers who worship her.'

Adunni yawned and rubbed her eyes with the palms of her hands, smudging her eye make-up. She wore almost as much of it as Elizabeth Taylor.

'I need to return to my studio. Can you take me to Ibokun Road, please?'

On the drive back we passed a trader sitting at a junction beside a heap of carved elephants he was trying to sell; this was Adunni's cue to fill me in about another primary *orisha*: Obatala.

Often depicted as an elephant, at one time, she explained with a chuckle, this god had a bit of an alcohol problem. According to the myth, Obatala moulded humans from earth, but one day he got drunk on palm wine and some of them came out crippled, albino and blind. When he sobered up he decided to quit the booze and care for the sick and disabled.

'Obatala has become what you might call a father figure to the Yoruba gods. He's renowned for his wisdom and compassion.'

'A wounded healer?'

'Yes, you could describe him as that. Now alcohol is forbidden to his followers. They wear white to symbolise purity.'

I thought about my Buddhist doctor friend, Boye; as a young man he'd had a somewhat rocky past. These days, when this compassionate man wasn't caring for the sick and disabled, like Obatala, he was doing research into herbs and plants which could be used for medicinal purposes. I began to grasp how the ability to identify with an *orisha*'s 'human' strengths and frailties – and even their gender flexibility – made them more accessible.

We drove to Ibokun Road in silence. I sensed there was something on Adunni's mind. She climbed out of the car and turned to go, then motioned to me to wind down my window. There was a note of agitation in her voice.

'I do respect the man.' I couldn't think who she was talking about.

'Jung, I mean. I respect Jung.' Ah! She was referring to our conversation earlier in the day.

'But you must understand that African wisdom runs deep; very deep. Even he came to that realisation. After his travels in India, Africa and New Mexico, Jung made it very clear that so-called 'primitive man' was by no means primitive; he was more in touch with the universe and his own psyche than 'civilised' western man.'

With that she turned away and strode off.

Not only had Adunni studied in depth the works of Marx, Freud, Jung and other great thinkers like Rudolf Steiner and Mircea Eliade, she regularly corresponded with Joseph Campbell, the twentieth century's most famous authority on religion, mythology and art. Her intellect and the extent of her reading thrilled me. I made up my mind, that day, to follow in her footsteps and embrace spheres of learning I'd never, hitherto, explored.

Harmattan

WE WERE walking towards the taxi rank at a crossroads near her house when Adunni began to cough.

'I do not feel so well. I will not work for long today. This sand affects my lungs.'

It was the season of the Harmattan; the fierce wind that blows the sands of the Sahara across much of West Africa, blocking out the sun and giving breathing problems to many.

'This can be an unforgiving land,' she wheezed, between fierce bouts of coughing. I looked around, in vain, for a taxi.

'Do you want to sit down somewhere? Or even go back home?'

She shook her head. A battered old Austin eventually pulled up beside the kerb. The taxi driver, who recognised Adunni, leapt out and held the door open for her – but not for me. As we drove through the town she stared out of the car window, occasionally lifting her hand in a regal gesture to the odd passerby who waved at her.

The driver dropped us off at the Sacred Groves but refused to take money from either of us.

'Dis groves lamentable…lamentable, Madam, before you done come here dey fix dem.' His bloodshot, malarial eyes glazed over in gratitude.

The driver turned to me by way of explanation. 'De gods dey forsaken dis place. Priests dey all done go.'

Adunni bowed her head and lightly touched his hand. 'Thank you, my friend.'

'We *orisha* people, we grateful for you for we can go pray now…and I get more business from peoples dey come look dere.'

Adunni shuddered slightly. 'Tourists. Please do not bring me too many of them.' The driver looked at me, confused. I felt myself blush.

Adunni reassured him, 'This young lady is not a tourist.' I smiled, gratefully.

Now that word had got around that the Sacred Groves had been regenerated and some fabulous 'sculptures' were on display, art tourists, who viewed it simply as an exhibition space, and curious travellers passing through, who sometimes left rubbish behind, were fast becoming one of Adunni's latest headaches.

We waited until the Austin was out of sight, and then walked a little way until we came to a clearing, where she sat on a fallen tree trunk and tried to get her breath back.

'Are you surprised,' I asked, 'that your School of New Sacred Art has started to attract international attention?'

'Not particularly. It is about time the world opened its eyes to what we in Africa have to offer. African religious art flourished long before the Cross or the Crescent made their regrettable appearance on this continent, you know.'

'I didn't, actually.'

'I have never understood,' she continued, 'why so-called "advanced" societies, or the cultures they drag along behind them, think themselves or their art superior to our own here in Africa.'

Snorting with disgust, she railed on about the damage perpetrated a hundred years earlier by the German ethnologist Leo Froebinius. After chancing upon the magnificent sculpted bronze heads and terracotta figures of Ilé-Ifè, Froebinius had insisted that such 'primitive' people didn't have the skill to produce these beautiful works of art.

'Idiot! Idiot!' Adunni shook her head angrily. 'He put forward the absurd theory that black Africa must have been conquered at some point by a whiter race of Mediterranean origin. He even had the cheek to call our ancient kingdom of Ilé-Ifè the lost Atlantis.'

'No-one believed him, surely?'

'Of course they did,' she snapped. 'Even though experts proved him wrong when more art of this calibre was discovered in 1938. There are some who still believe him, just as they believe Auschwitz and Belsen never existed.'

But it wasn't only ignorant old ethnologists and messy, secular tourists who riled Adunni. In common with Ifa adherents down the centuries who have found themselves up against an assortment of hostile slave masters, missionaries, racists, fundamentalists and rival factions, she, too, had had numerous sets of saboteurs to deal with.

'The problems I have had here in these groves, and continue to have, are exhausting,' she sighed, 'but I never lose heart. Any project of value will naturally attract opposition; some of it vicious…'

A lizard darted through the long grass.

'These poachers camouflage themselves like that lizard. They even catch the poor creatures for food.' I tried not to imagine what lizard might taste like.

'It has been taboo for centuries to steal or destroy anything that lives on or grows in this sacred land, but poachers still try to hunt and fish here, and chop down the ancient trees for firewood.'

'There are poachers in Lagos, too,' I offered. 'Our steward's pet monkey was stolen last week. Apparently she ended up in the cooking pot of a Hauser night-watchman who works a couple of doors down. My son was heartbroken. He and the monkey used to play with his *Star Wars* toys together. The poor monkey was terrified of Darth Vader.' Adunni looked at me blankly; she hadn't heard of Star Wars. Our worlds felt far apart.

I was anxious to change the subject. 'Tell me about the other problems you have here. Do the local church and mosque-goers object to you holding Ifa rituals?'

'Some still do, yes, but in the beginning it was much worse. Christian and Muslim religious fanatics joined forces with property developers.' She pointed to Oshun's shrine a few metres away. 'Some years ago I had to sit down in front of the Iyemowoo shrine to prevent a fool in a bulldozer from destroying it.'

'Iyemowoo? I thought that was Oshun's shrine.'

'It is. Iyemowoo means sacrosanct womb of the goddess: the place of birth into another dimension of reality.'

'Ah.' I pictured her, a lone woman, sat at the shrine's vagina-shaped entrance, determined to protect the sacred feminine from bellicose he-man bulldozers.

'They wanted to clear the Groves of our shrines so that they could build on the land. But they knew they would have to murder me first. It was a battle of wills.'

'Weren't you afraid?'

'No. Just angry. Oshun would never allow them to harm me.'

I was moved by the depth of her faith in her goddess. 'But I was devastated when local chiefs banned me from coming to the Sacred Groves.'

'Banned you? Why?'

'I shall show you.'

She led me through the trees to a magnificent, androgynous carving of a slender, naked figure which stood several metres high, its arms stretching up to the heavens.

'They objected to the nudity of this sculpture. They said it shamed the gods.'

In an early photograph I'd seen of this shrine to Ela – the *orisha* of peace – the figure had an erect penis. I asked Adunni why it was now missing.

'My enemies hired a group of thugs to go on the rampage one night with their machetes. They attacked our shrines and hacked off arms and sex organs.'

There was something poignantly symbolic about this infantile dismemberment. Adunni was single and childless. How lonely it must be for her, I thought, dealing, on her own, with such hostility and desecration.

Dangerous Waters

ADUNNI'S courage was inspiring. Towards the end of that Nigerian visit an opportunity arose for me to test my courage, too. But it couldn't have come at a worse time.

I was having a drink in the Ikoyi Club when an expat I'd met a few times came over and asked if he could join me. We started off chatting about a Live Aid scandal which was unravelling. Some of the food and clothing destined for famine-stricken Ethiopia had been diverted to Nigeria by corrupt middlemen and was being sold off in Lagos market. The expat then went on to tell me about another, lesser-known racket: a group of wealthy Nigerians, in cahoots with what was then the Soviet Union, were importing meat from the Chernobyl region of Ukraine and flooding the market with it. Declared unfit for consumption elsewhere in the world, the cheap meat had been contaminated by radiation following Chernobyl's 1986 nuclear disaster; a poisoned chalice for the many Nigerians for whom meat was a rare luxury.

The expat, like many who had been in Nigeria too long, was a hardened cynic and thought it all a bit of a joke – the irony being that African uranium had launched the world into the nuclear orbit in the first place. The first American nuclear reactor had been built with uranium from Zaire.

I hardly slept that night, trying to decide whether or not I should act on this chilling information. I was flying back to the UK in a couple of days; if I did decide to do something, what on earth could I possibly do?

The following day I travelled down to Oshogbo to interview Adunni for what would be the last time before submitting the final draft of my documentary proposal. I'd made up my mind not to tell her about the meat business. I had a pretty clear idea what her response would be, but I wasn't ready to deal with it.

We were walking through the Sacred Groves, heading in the direction of Oshun's shrine, when she bent down and picked up a round object that resembled a potato.

'Try it,' she said, wiping it on her smock and handing it to me. I took a bite – the taste was bitter-sweet, but not unpleasant. 'What is it?'

'The fruit of this tree.' She pointed up at the fulsome, leafy tree towering over us. 'It's a marula; the fruit isn't poisonous,' she ran her hand down the tree's gnarled old trunk, 'but people are fearful of it.'

'Why?'

'It has a reputation for driving elephants mad.' I looked at her, quizzically. 'When they eat the fermented fruit the elephants become inebriated. Some herds cross miles of savannah in search of marulas.'

I laughed at the idea of mad, drunk elephants, and of the herd nursing a collective hangover the following morning.

'I doubt you would find it so amusing if they were trampling down your village,' she said with a smile, breaking open a piece of fruit. 'The nut inside is nutritional and has healing properties. For thousands of years Africans have been harvesting marula nuts for their health.'

She picked up more pieces of the fruit and stuffed them into her pockets. I looked away; a wave of nausea had come over me as I compared this ancient, nutritious fruit with the noxious, radioactive meat. Oblivious to its toxicity, poor Africans would make a beeline for this cheap, contaminated meat with the same gusto that elephant herds foraged for marula fruit.

We continued walking in the direction of the shrine. I stopped in my tracks when we reached the river. Something green and shiny on the river bed had caught my eye. I took off my sandals and waded into the shallows.

'The water's so calm and clear,' I enthused, as I bent down to pick up a strangely-shaped pebble.

Adunni smiled. 'Oshun knows she is loved and worshipped in these groves… Further downstream it is quite a different story…'

I rolled the pebble around in my hand and held it up to the light. Suddenly excited, I waved it at Adunni.

'This is jade, isn't it?'

'Yes, but you must put it back. You may *not* keep it.'

'But my son and I have a pebble collection back in London…'

'You may not keep it.' Annoyed, Adunni shook her head at me. 'I have discussed with you the evils of poaching. *Everything* in the river and in these groves belongs to Oshun.'

I blushed. I'd never considered myself a poacher.

'She demands respect for women and she demands it for

nature. It is wise not to cross her.' Registering my embarrassment, her voice softened slightly. 'As the river approaches the rapids she becomes wild and untameable – manifesting the goddess's tyrannical aspect when crossed. People drown.'

'OK – thanks for warning me.' Reluctantly, I chucked Oshun's diaphanous pebble back into the water.

'Gold, indigo, ivory, diamonds, sapphires, uranium, petroleum, iron ore, copper, lead, zinc, jade – so much has been taken from Africa,' Adunni was on a roll. 'And that is before we take into account the precious lives captured, tortured and killed in slavery, or the magnificent wildlife slaughtered not for survival but for pleasure.'

Adunni's rant brought home to me how much good stuff we extract from Africa, and how, when it all goes wrong – like a nuclear reactor breaking down – we offload the detritus onto them.

'No wonder Oshun's anger is so volcanic.'

'Oshun is enraged only when she witnesses disrespect and injustice, but do not forget the essence of the goddess is love.' We sat on a patch of dry grass by the river, sipping water, as Adunni recounted the goddess's role in the Ifa creation myth.

She explained how a few rather cheeky, primordial male *orisha* had tried to construct the earth without the help of a female *orisha*. They failed miserably in their task because they kept Oshun, aka Love, out of the equation. The goddess became a ringleader, gathering together other female energies to protest about this to Oludomare, the chief divinity. He ruled that the goddess must have a hand in the work, too. It wasn't until the primordial males included Oshun in the task that Creation itself was made whole.

Back in Lagos that night, I discovered a handful of marula fruit in the bottom of my rucksack; a farewell gift from Adunni. She must have slipped it in when I wasn't looking. When I gave the fruit to the steward his face lit up. I had a heart-sink moment as I remembered the radioactive meat. What if he were to buy some of it in Lagos market and feed it to his kids?

What had struck me most about the creation myth I'd heard that afternoon was that Oshun hadn't let those guys get away with it. She'd had the balls to *speak out* about their disrespect and injustice. I made up my mind, then and there, that I would do something about the contaminated meat business. I wasn't going to speak out about it to Oludomare. I decided, instead, to tell my DJ journalist friend, Ebis.

Colour-blind

BACK HOME in London the news reached me that Ebis had been arrested, without charge, and thrown into prison.

I'd met up with him just before leaving Nigeria and told him all I knew about the meat racket; he must have acted on the information immediately. He'd had the temerity – or stupidity – to broadcast multiple warnings on his popular radio shows. I assumed, correctly as it transpired, that 'the big boys' were behind his arrest – but these were much bigger boys than he was used to exposing. Why had he put himself so directly in the firing line? Surely he could have disseminated the information in a less robust manner. Ebis had always wanted a closer relationship with me than I felt capable of offering. I tormented myself with the thought that this was, perhaps, a misguided attempt, on his part, to somehow prove himself.

Guilt tormented me. I was no Oshun, standing up to the primordial males, or Adunni, sitting in front of a bulldozer. I'd dumped the radioactive meat story on *him*. Like my colonial forebears, I'd waded in without considering the consequences of my actions and then schlepped off home to safe old England.

To give me my due, once I'd acknowledged this, I tried, without success, to do my bit, too. I approached a number of British newspapers but none were interested in the meat scandal or Ebis' arrest, because, they said, it didn't involve Britain or Brits. Amnesty International was sympathetic, but needed more information about his detention before they could commit to any involvement.

I spent a fortune on phone calls to my eldest sister, Sue, who was living in the Solomon Islands – my wise, compassionate 'go to' person in times of need. She'd spent a couple of years in Nigeria when her partner was working in Port Harcourt; she knew how the country worked.

'Give yourself a break,' Sue tried to reassure me. 'It was Ebis' decision to make those announcements; they probably saved lives.'

Meanwhile, the reaction to my documentary proposal, *Suzanne and her Goddess*, was also causing me grief. The script unit liked it and showed it to a couple of producers within the BBC but I was taken aback by the response I received. The gist of it seemed to be that Adunni was the wrong colour to be 'dabbling' in African culture, and so was I, to be writing about it. Another response – from a female producer, too – was that, as a woman, my writing should be more focused on what was happening at home, what I was 'familiar with', rather than straying into 'foreign territory'.

These patronising and parochial responses greatly frustrated me. I'd hoped, by demonstrating the depth and complexity of this ancient belief system, to illuminate the absurdity of the notion of white superiority which was still fuelling apartheid in South Africa, and racism in other parts of the world. Adunni wasn't a western missionary trying to impose her beliefs on the Yoruba; she was pouring all her energy and resources into assisting them in the regeneration of their ancient faith, which had been all but decimated by colonial missionaries and administrators; a faith that she'd found so universal and profound she'd come to embrace it herself.

I later learnt that a BBC news crew based in Africa had already attempted to interview her. She'd sent them packing because she wasn't in the mood, that day, to receive visitors. This came as no surprise. It also made me appreciate how privileged I was to have spent time with her.

A few months later, Sacha and I returned to Nigeria for what would be our last trip there for the foreseeable future, as Roberto had been asked to take on a major architectural project in Paris. I wasn't looking forward to seeing either Adunni or Ebis; I felt I'd let them both down.

Ebis spent three months in prison without being charged. I met up with him not long after his release. When the taxi dropped me off at his new address in the Lagos suburb of Ebute-Meta, a much thinner Ebis was waiting for me outside.

'So what happened to your last place?' I was confused. Instead of his suburban bungalow situated in a middle-class area, he was now living in a run-down neighbourhood, in one of many small rooms in a scruffy building with one communal bathroom.

'They decided to teach me a lesson.' He laughed, attempting to make light of it. 'When I returned home from prison, my home was no longer there. It had been burnt to the ground, along with all my possessions.'

'The bastards... I'm so, so sorry...'

Ebis went on to describe his hellish time inside the jail. To avoid getting his throat cut he'd had to spend most of the day and night in a filthy, overcrowded, sweltering cell, fanning a hardened criminal boss.

'I do not regret it.' His voice was sincere. 'We saved lives.'

Mindful of his safety, Ebis began taking work assignments out of Lagos whenever he could. I accompanied him on one of these. We flew to Joss, in the north, in a plane with broken seat belts and a pair of goats wandering up the central aisle, to meet a very wealthy businessman who wanted Ebis to undertake some PR work. Oozing self-importance, the corpulent, boastful, married businessman, with his über-opulent home and sleazy entourage of skin-bleached mistresses, did not appeal to me. I feared he was yet another fat-cat 'big boy'.

I avoided visiting Adunni until the very end of that trip. When I arrived she was peeling a mango on her terrace, in the shade of a bougainvillea. A couple of barefoot kids in underpants were jumping up and down the steps, clapping their hands in laughter. She smiled at them benevolently. An old goat wandered over to chew on the peel. When she saw me, she motioned for to me to sit beside her.

I pulled up a stool and recounted the sorry tale of the failed proposal and the irritating feedback.

'The *orisha* are universal property,' she sighed. 'I have as much right as anyone to worship them.' I had the feeling this was a phrase she had to repeat on a regular basis.

'Doesn't it hurt,' I asked, 'when you hear these negative comments about your involvement with Yoruba culture?'

She shrugged her shoulders. 'I have grown accustomed to

criticism from so-called intellectuals – black and white – for many years now. Post-colonial era Afro-centrists resent a white woman being a catalyst in the revival of an archaic culture; white ethnologists accuse me of hijacking that same culture.'

'But we have so much to learn from one another.'

Adunni nodded in agreement. 'Like any religion of value it shouldn't matter where it is practised or who it is practised by. These people just want to isolate African culture – which is another way of demeaning it – denying its importance and relevance to world culture.'

One by one, she beckoned the children over and handed them each a slice of mango.

'Thank-you, Mamma,' they chanted, in unison.

'I feel I am part of the Yoruba culture, not because I think I have changed into a black person or a traditional Yoruba, but through a spontaneous, deep understanding of what the *orisha* represent.'

'I understand that, Adunni, I really do.'

'Do you? Do you *really* understand what they represent?' Her tone was sharp. 'Buddhism originated in India,' she continued. 'I don't hear anyone complaining that the Dalai Lama shouldn't be practising it.' She turned to face me. 'Or you, for that matter.'

I must have looked upset, because her voice softened.

'This project of yours will happen if you really want it to...' She gazed into the distance as if surveying the future. '...But perhaps not in the way or at the time you might wish it to.'

A youngish guy in a white *agbada* and matching *fila*, with a drum tucked under his arm, strode through the gate and crouched in the corner. Adunni nodded at him and he began tapping softly on the drum.

'Is that a talking drum?' I asked her.

'It is.'

'You understand what it's saying, don't you?

'Of course I understand what the drum is saying!'

The kids and the old goat seemed to understand, too. But Adunni wasn't going to share the drum's mysteries with uninitiated little me. I looked on as she and the drummer held one another's gaze. And in that moment I realised that a documentary was of little interest to her. What she'd really wanted was for me to become more deeply involved in Oshun; to participate in rituals.

Ebis eventually found permanent work in another city. We rarely met again after that. He never held me responsible for his decline in fortune, but I did. I was left with a lingering sense of guilt.

And as for Adunni, it would be another ten years before I saw her again.

Wild Swimming

SALLY WAS excited. My younger sister had been living in Nigeria for five years but this would be her first time in Oshogbo. Also an artist, she'd heard a great deal about Adunni and the Sacred Groves, not just from me but also from fellow artists and friends she'd made in the Goethe Institute in Lagos.

I'd flown into the country two days earlier. A small production company in London had recently contacted me to see if I had any interesting proposals up my sleeve. I raked through my bottom draw and pulled out a couple of projects. After the response *Suzanne and her Goddess* had received ten years earlier, I dithered over whether or not to include it. To my surprise, it was the one proposal the company were genuinely enthusiastic about. Needing to ensure the contents hadn't dated and that Adunni would still be a willing participant, they asked me to record an interview with her and shoot some rough video footage of the Sacred Groves. Delighted at the possibility that this treasured project might actually come off, I hadn't wasted any time purchasing my ticket.

On the outskirts of Oshogbo one of the front tyres burst. Sally's driver (the first she'd been able to afford) informed us there wasn't a spare, so we abandoned the car and legged it the rest of the way to our guesthouse. By the time we'd checked in and walked the considerable distance to Ibokun Road, it was already dark and a thunderstorm was raging.

Sally was hesitant. 'Don't you think it's a bit late to be calling on her?' She was right, of course, but I was keen to get it over with. This time around, I was concerned that Adunni might not remember me – and if she did, that she might send me packing.

'We're here now; there's no harm trying.' Against my better judgement I tapped on the door. Eventually it creaked open and Adunni peered around it. Wearing a fedora and shedloads of eye make-up, she looked more like a female version of Baron Samedi than a high priestess of Oshun. Sally instinctively took a step backwards. I held out my hand.

'Hello Adunni, do you remember me?'

She stared at me and my hand for what felt like an age and then nodded, slowly.

'Yes, but I cannot recall your name.' I reminded her, briefly. Limply, she shook my hand. I introduced Sally.

'Your sister? Looks nothing like you.'

Adunni was right. Not only was Sally ten years my junior, she was light-haired, unlike me, and, at the time, considerably underweight for her height. The cheekbones in her attractive face had become too prominent; her complexion was sallow and there were dark rings under her eyes.

Seven years earlier, Boye, my doctor friend, had asked if I'd like to support the Nigerian Buddhists with their staging of a Wole Soyinka play. I put it to Sally, who had just completed a masters in art at the Slade, that it would be fun for her to come

over, too, and help out with painting the set. Udo, the Nigerian
directing the play was also a handsome and talented dancer and
actor. He and Sally fell in love. They stayed in touch when she
returned to England. Two years later she decided to up sticks
and move to Africa. This didn't go down well with my parents;
neither did the surprise announcement that, shortly after her
arrival, she'd married in a hurry because she needed a work visa.

Sally handed Adunni the bottle of decent duty-free scotch I'd
invested in at Heathrow. She examined the label.

'Come back tomorrow, in the afternoon,' she growled, and
slammed the door in our faces. Sally turned to me, her eyebrows
raised. I shrugged my shoulders, apologetically. We hurried back
to the guest house in torrential rain.

'Yes, she can come across as a bit weird', I said, pre-empting
Sally's thoughts as we laboured over a lukewarm supper of
pounded yam and hot pepper soup.

'Weird! That's putting it mildly! She was terrifying. The
thunder and lightning didn't help.'

'She's aged more than I'd anticipated. I guess she must be
around eighty now. You were right. We should have waited until
the morning.

Sally gulped back some water. 'Well, at least she didn't tell us
to piss off and never come back.'

The following morning we were woken by loud banging on
our guestroom door. The driver had found a replacement tyre
and needed some *naire* to pay for it. Once the tyre was fixed
we drove to the Sacred Groves in silence. Sally was suffering
from exhaustion and an as yet undiagnosed stomach problem. I
couldn't help but compare how vibrant, happy and healthy my

sister had looked when she'd set off for her new life in Nigeria, five years earlier.

Only days after she'd arrived, Sally had been offered a job teaching art at former president General Olesegun Obasanjo's newly-founded school for girls in the Lagos suburb of Ota. Appointed Head of State in 1976, Obasanjo had ruled for three years until he did the decent thing and became the first military leader to transfer power to a democratically elected civilian president.

Sally and Udo lived with Obasanjo on his farm while they were waiting for their accommodation to become available.

The general, who always wandered around the farm in a bath towel, also shared his home with his pet goat and a Buddhist monk who wanted to erect a peace pagoda in Nigeria. Sally practises the same Buddhism as I do, and, by coincidence, the month she arrived in Nigeria, our Buddhist magazine, *SGI Graphic*, had on its cover a picture of the general in dialogue with Daisaku Ikeda, the president of our organisation, on the subject of peace. Sally felt reassured she'd landed in the right place.

A year or so later she held a prestigious exhibition, opened by the general, and was finally able to give up her teaching job. Her art began selling well and she and Udo decided to move back into central Lagos. They lived, for a time, at Jazz 38 with Fran Kuboye, Fela Kuti's jazz-singer niece, and her bass-playing partner, Tunde. A ramshackle venue, which also housed Fran's dental practice and their living quarters, Jazz 38 was a favourite haunt of Nigerian and expat music lovers. The jerry-built club had an open-air stage, a corrugated tin roof, a concrete floor and patio chairs and tables, but the music was great, the beer cheap and it rocked. Life was stimulating and fun. Inspired by the arty, musical community they found themselves part of, Sally and

Udo decided to set up their own arts company.

The general had developed an avuncular fondness for Sally, and once she and her partner had found a place of their own, he became a frequent visitor. I met him there a couple of times, and was also invited for dinner at his farm. For Sally, it was reassuring to know that a Nigerian of influence, like Obasanjo, had her back. But recently the political tide had turned, and now, at a time when she most needed security, her patron was in deep water himself.

In the intervening years I'd learnt a great deal more about the political maelstrom that is Nigerian politics and the danger the coup-happy military elite posed to any would-be democratic politician. In London I'd made friends with Sadik Balewa, the filmmaker son of Nigeria's first post-independence prime minister, Sir Abubakar Tafawa Balewa. Sadik had told me how, after hearing there had been a military coup in the South in 1966, he and his mother and siblings, who lived in the northern Nigerian state of Bauchi, waited in desperation for news of his father. They were jubilant when his mother finally received a phone call to say her husband was on the next plane home. They rushed to the airport to meet him. The kids chatted excitedly together as they waited on the tarmac for the plane to land. But this time their father didn't step out of the plane and wave at them all, as was his custom. He was carried down the steps of the plane in a wooden box. His body had been discovered at a roadside near Lagos six days after he was ousted from office.

I'd also got to know the widow of the former Head of State, General Murtala Mohammed, who was assassinated in an abortive coup attempt in 1976, at the young age of thirty-seven, by fellow officers who opposed his war on corruption. Mrs Mohammed had once invited me to spend the day with her on her farm in the country. She was an impressive woman:

intelligent, yet humble; deeply religious, but no zealot. Our trip was during Ramadan, and despite the intense heat, not a drop of water passed her lips as she was fasting. In the fourteen hours we spent together she never once complained of thirst – or of anything for that matter. The only time she expressed distaste was when she told me that one of the National Museum's most popular exhibits was the bullet-ridden, black Mercedes Benz saloon car her husband was assassinated in. Even today, it attracts thousands of visitors each month.

The current de-facto Nigerian president, when Sally and I were in Oshogbo, was General Sani Abacha. He'd recently thrown the newly democratically elected civilian president, Moshood Abiola, into prison following the latter's landside victory, and had ordered the assassination of Abiola's wife. Earlier in the year, the 1996 UN fact-finding mission hadn't minced its words: *Nigeria's problems of human rights are terrible and the political problems are terrifying.* The report went on to accuse the Abacha government of embezzling a billion US dollars-worth of public funds into private bank accounts in Europe and the Persian Gulf.

Eyeing Sally's former boss, General Obasanjo, as a potential threat, Abacha had falsely accused him of plotting a coup, and sentenced him to life in prison. Only recently, while being transferred to another prison, Obasanjo had narrowly avoided an assassination attempt. Under the pretence of testing his cholesterol, a 'doctor' tried to give him a lethal injection. Obasanjo's former deputy head of state, who had been arrested with him, wasn't so lucky. Needless to say, all this weighed heavily on my sister, and was impacting on her health.

Sally's colour returned the minute we entered the Sacred Groves.

'There's a real vibe in this place.' She clutched my arm, overwhelmed by the sheer beauty of the shrines and the wildlife and nature that surrounded them. 'I can feel spirits or powerful energies around… I've never seen anything like it…'

'Come on,' I said, taking her by the hand. 'We don't have much time. I want to show you the Oshun River.'

Sunlight sparkled on the rivulets of water. No one was around – just the odd goddess or two. Both keen swimmers, my sister and I could read each other's mind.

'Shall we?' Sally nodded. We stripped down to our underwear and waded into the river. The only sound we could hear was the chirping of crickets, birdsong and the leaves of the trees being rustled by monkeys. Silver fish leapt around us as we swam in the clear, shallow waters.

Afterwards we lay on the river bank and dried ourselves in the sun. Sally closed her eyes. 'I don't want to go back to Lagos… ever… The shrines, the river, the rainforest – it's all sublime.'

I was beginning to drift off when a weaver bird flew just above my head, flapping its wings noisily. I glanced at my watch and leapt up.

'Christ! Get dressed quick, or we'll be late for Adunni.'

Red Sky at Night

WHILE SALLY wandered from room to room, examining in detail the sculptures, carvings and batiks, the High Priestess and I sat on wooden stools in her studio, sipping Guinness out of chipped glasses. Adunni was more welcoming than she had been the previous evening. Perhaps because I'd grown in confidence myself I no longer found her so intimidating.

Adunni's School of New Sacred Art, had, by now, established a global reputation, and her cherished ambition to have the Sacred Groves declared a protected World Heritage site was under serious consideration. Although ambivalent, she didn't dismiss this possible second foray into a documentary being made.

I may not have seen her for a decade, but Adunni had never been far from my mind. The short time I'd spent in her company had, in a roundabout way, enabled me to smash through my own glass ceiling of what I could achieve both as a woman and as an artist. In the intervening years, I'd taken edgy performance art work beyond the UK to Europe and New York. Inspired by her intellectual curiosity, I'd researched and written a screenplay about a psychoanalyst which had won an award. A decent sum of money came with it, and an entrée into writing drama for television. Her boldness, when it came to embracing cultural and ethnic diversity in her work, encouraged me to take greater risks, and to pursue projects with a multi-cultural agenda. I scripted a Bollywood movie for the stage with an all-Asian cast, which won another award and toured the UK and Canada. But possibly my most courageous act – given my turbulent relationship history – had been to marry again. David, my new partner, didn't have a problem with me jetting off to Africa at a moment's notice, but he did object to living in London. I'd recently sold my flat and upped sticks to Brighton.

Sally wandered back into the studio, smiling.

'These carvings are some of the best I've seen over here.' Adunni looked her up and down. 'Your sister tells me you are an artist and that you are married to a Nigerian theatre director.'

'That's right, I am. He's from Akwa Ibom.'

'Would you like a little of this?' Adunni held up the bottle of Guinness.

'I'd better not, thanks, I'm under observation for a suspected ulcer.'

'Mmm. So what sort of an artist are you, then?'

'A printmaker, mainly. Over here, though, I work in oils and watercolour – mostly on commissions of African scenes for expats. It pays the bills. My partner and I also run a theatre and dance troupe; Iwana Arts. We've been touring Nigeria, Cameroon and other African countries with a play called *The Courageous Cry*. It's about human rights… We based it on a quotation from our Buddhist leader: *The courageous cry of even a single individual standing up for justice…can light a flame in the hearts of thousands and change the course of human history…'*

'She needs to be very careful.' Adunni was addressing me. There was concern in her voice. But Sally didn't need telling, and neither did I.

WHEN DUSK fell we moved our stools over to the studio window to admire the intense reds of the sunset.

'This crimson sky,' Adunni said in her throaty Germanic drawl, 'it brings to mind the evening before *Anschluss.*'

'*Anschluss*?' I queried.

'The annexation of Austria…'

'Hitler?'

She nodded. 'He and his troops marched in to stop the referendum which was being held to determine whether we wanted to become part of the Third Reich. He knew the Austrian people would vote to keep their independence…'

'Were you there at the time?' Ignoring my question she continued, '…A month later, Hitler held his own referendum to prove to the world that we were happy with German control. It was rigged of course. Each vote was monitored.'

She poured herself some more Guinness and stared out at the sky. I could detect tears in her eyes.

'The night before the troops arrived, vastly different shades of red appeared across the sky as the sun was setting… My studio, which was on the eighth floor of the Vienna Karlsplatz, had a skylight. We – myself and a few friends – looked up at the sky on fire and down on the packs of deranged young Nazis running around the square below… It was madness, pure madness.'

Adunni stood up and began pacing the room. 'A friend of mine, another artist, was with us that evening, watching the sunset… He had deserted from the front. After *Anschluss* he hid in my apartment. One day he painted a beautiful picture…then he decided to give himself up and was shot.'

I looked at my sister. There were tears in her eyes, too.

'It's strange,' Sally said, 'how red sky seems to be a harbinger of death. On the day they hanged Ken Saro-Wiwa the sky was streaked with red. I knew he'd been executed.'

Sally and her partner had been friends with the prominent human rights campaigner, Ken Saro-Wiwa, who, only a year earlier, had been hanged by a military court. Saro-Wiwa had campaigned tirelessly on behalf of the Ogoni people of Niger Delta against Shell Oil's widespread polluting of Ogoniland. His execution, for supporting the Ogonis' peaceful uprising against Shell, had sparked international outrage, and led to Nigeria's suspension from the Commonwealth.

'Saro-Wiwa was a brave man; a good man,' Adunni sighed. 'A lion savaged by a pack of greedy hyenas.'

'What was it like,' Sally asked Adunni, 'being an artist under the Nazi regime?'

'If you possessed an ounce of integrity it was impossible to be what I would call an artist – or you, most probably.' Adunni turned to face Sally. 'I was branded a degenerate artist, young woman. I had to paint in secret.' She laughed, but her laughter was hollow.

'At least I got to see some exceptional art. The Nazi Ministry of Propaganda organised a touring exhibition – *Entartete Kunst* – Degenerate Art. It included anything abstract or expressionist; by a communist or a Jew; against war and militarism. I got to see over 650 works of 'degenerate' art, including the Cubists and Dadaists and paintings by many of my favourite artists, like Kandinsky, Klee and Mondrian. Thanks to Hitler, I also heard the music of Schoenberg for the first time. It was the most inspiring exhibition I and many others had ever seen.'

I turned to Sally. 'If you'd been alive then, your work would have been in that exhibition, too.' Under the current climate, Sally and her partner's links with both Saro-Wiwa and Obasanjo were dangerous. Iwana Arts was starting to attract attention from the wrong quarters.

While Sally showed Adunni some slides of her work, I took out my camera, hoping to catch a shot of this glorious Oshogbo sunset. Leaning against the barber's shop on the other side of the street, smoking a cigarette, was the same chubby guy in jeans and a check shirt I'd seen hanging around outside our guesthouse that morning. He looked up at the window and caught my eye. I moved quickly away.

Igbeyawo

FILMING in the Sacred Groves was a nightmare. The battery on the camera was so useless I had to hire a generator. Old, noisy and cumbersome, it was too heavy for Sally to carry. At Adunni's suggestion, a priest and priestess of Oshun agreed to help us out.

Patient, energetic and good-natured, the young married couple were both dressed from head to toe in white. He carried the generator and she insisted, despite our protestations, on helping us with our rucksacks.

We stopped for lunch on a patch of grass under the shade of a tree beside the river bank. Once we'd finished eating a lunch of fried plantain and *akara* – bean cakes – the priestess offered to give us a cowrie-shell reading.

She unravelled her white head wrapper and laid it out on the grass. Taking sixteen white shells from a pouch at her side – each one symbolising a principal *orisha* – she threw them onto the wrapper.

The couple studied them intently for a few moments, then whispered to each other in Yoruba. Based on the positions the shells had landed in, they proceeded to interpret each divination.

Children are considered a blessing in Nigeria. Sally, who was experiencing a certain amount of pressure in this area, wanted to know whether she would ever have any. The issue of children concerned me; since arriving in the country I'd been feeling uneasy about the state of her marriage.

On the journey down to Oshogbo, Sally had been chatting about her recent initiation as an honorary member of the Ekpe Society in Akwa Ibom.

'I was the first white woman allowed to join the society,' she told me, proudly. 'It was a real honour.'

'It certainly was. Ekpe means Peacock Leopard, doesn't it?'

'Leopard Peacock.'

So what was involved in this initiation, then?'

'Dancing; speechmaking. The drumming got really loud. When it reached a crescendo they killed this little goat in my honour... I felt terrible.' She gave me a sideways glance. 'I'm no vegetarian, like you, but I couldn't face eating it...'

'How could you avoid it, though – given it was slaughtered in your honour?'

'Once the meat was cooked I told them I wanted to retire to my room so that I could properly savour the dish and reflect upon the honour they'd bestowed upon me. When I got there I chucked the goat meat out of the window.'

Looking glum, Sally continued. 'During the initiation celebrations, you know who got really pissed on palm wine. It was still morning. I hate that...the amount of it he drinks every time we go back to the village… If you drink palm wine in the evening when it's much stronger, more fermented, you're considered an alkie by the locals. In the morning it's still light. So he just drinks a load more…'

I reminded her that when she first moved to Nigeria, *Iquoma* – she who brings sunshine to the party – was the African name conferred upon her by Ibibio and Efik elders. Sally smiled, wistfully.

'After that naming ceremony we all sat beside the Niger River and drank schnapps from Shippam's fish-paste pots… That all seems a long, long time ago, now.'

Earlier that morning of the filming, as I was setting up my tape recorder to interview Adunni in the studio, I'd overheard her speaking to Sally in a lowered voice.

'*Igbeyawo* – marriage – to a Nigerian is not the same as marriage to a European, my dear.'

Sally looked startled. 'This is the only time I've been married, so I have nothing to compare it with.'

'There are usually more than just two of you for a start.'

I strained my ears to catch what she was saying. I'd never dared question Adunni much about her relationships.

Sally shook her head. 'I don't think he's like that, but…'

'Well,' Adunni gave Sally a wry smile, 'I have had the good fortune – and misfortune – to have been married to both…and divorced from both.'

Adunni and Ulli's 'European' marriage began to fall apart when they moved to Oshogbo. She set about pouring her life into restoring the shrines and creating new ones. Ulli, who was more interested in the cultural aspects of Yoruba life than the religious, was away for much of the time, travelling around the countryside collecting folktales and poetry. A prolific writer on African art and literature, he founded *Black Orpheus* – the first African literary journal in English, which was to have a powerful influence on the independence movement. He also edited the first *Penguin Book of Modern African Poetry*. With such divergent and all-consuming interests, they had little time – or energy – left over for one another.

Ulli met a London artist called Georgina Betts. For a while the three of them occupied different floors of the same Oshogbo house – a set-up which can't have been without its tensions. In time, Georgina became Ulli's second wife.

'And, sadly, for many Europeans,' Adunni continued, 'marriage to a Nigerian ends in divorce.'

She later fell in love with Chief Ayonsola Oniru Alarape, a famous, non-English-speaking Yoruba drummer. His powerful drumming affected her on a deep level during Ifa rituals. They became lovers. When it came to sharing the awe and intensity of the religious experience they were on the same page. He, however, already had a wife and children.

Polygamous marriage is traditional in Yoruba culture, and Adunni knowingly entered into one with Ayonsola. She had a good relationship with his wife and children, who became like her own. But a true Yoruba marriage involved mutual respect and an acknowledgement of the independence of all parties involved. Over time, however, Ayonsola became controlling and jealous. In the end, she tired of his desire to dominate her and demanded a divorce.

'There really are just the two of us in my marriage,' Sally insisted, defensively.

'Then I wish you well'. Adunni turned away and walked towards me. 'Are you ready?'

Sally was relieved to be told by the priest and priestess that, according to the cowrie shells, she would, in the future, have two children. As for me, they insisted that I was a queen. This was news to me at the time, but made sense retrospectively, when I discovered that Oshun, who is often portrayed as a queen, was my guardian *orisha*. The priest and priestess also told me that I would have followers. I'm still waiting…

Stalker

We decided to leave a few days earlier than planned. For almost a week we'd been followed around Oshogbo. Our pursuer never changed his check shirt or jeans; either this was his undercover outfit or he'd run out of washing powder. But we were both pretty sure he'd been commandeered into keeping an eye on my 'activist' sister, and/or was after a bribe of some sort. We tried to kid ourselves that we wouldn't let him put a damper on Sally's much-needed break or my precious time with Adunni, but it wasn't working.

The high priestess had mentioned on a previous visit that she was very fond of Alsace wine, which is made in the German tradition; Austrian and German wines were pretty much impossible to find in Nigeria at the time. I managed to pick up a bottle from a supermarket in Ibadan – no expense spared. We took it along with us the evening we went to say our goodbyes.

Adunni was agitated. She'd been without electricity all day. A couple of German art collectors were due the following morning and she was attempting to tidy up her studio – not an easy task in candlelight. We offered to help. While Adunni put away tools, Sally rinsed paintbrushes and I dusted dead moths and flies from sculptures and canvases.

Once we'd finished clearing up, we sat around a table chewing cola nuts and sipping Alsace wine out of plastic beakers. Adunni wanted to know why we were leaving early. When I told her about our stalker Sally tried to make light of it.

'We've grown so used to him following us that a couple of times we've smiled at him and waved.'

'And he examines his nails,' I added, 'or just turns away and lights a cigarette.' Adunni opened the window and peered out. She shook her head; there was no sign of him.

'You must take care,' she whispered, hoarsely. 'It isn't a joke.'

'I know.' Sally bit her lip. 'But laughter helps me keep a handle on the fear.'

'I understand,' Adunni's voice softened. 'When the terror is there, it is all you are able to do sometimes… I did the same when I joined up with the Resistance.'

'You were part of the Resistance…in the war?' I couldn't hide the excitement in my voice. This woman had lived so many lives.

'The Austrian Resistance… I hid people on the run – strangers; Jews, mainly. I washed the shit off their clothes. I didn't ask questions.'

'You were taking a huge risk…' She fixed her gaze on me.

'I couldn't just stand by and watch so many innocent people being transported away. It is what any decent person would have done.'

'Any decent *and* incredibly brave person.'

She shrugged her shoulders. 'I enjoyed a good rapport with the Jews in our city. The poor souls were forced to inhabit a so-called 'voluntary' ghetto in Vienna's Second District…'

There was a faraway look in her eyes '...And then they took away Lany...'

'Who was Lany?'

'A genius; Lany was a genius. He discovered Kokoschka and Schiele...'

Sally's ears pricked up. 'God, I love those artists.'

'...Lany was drawn to artists like bees to wild roses. He took me under his wing. On the upper floor of his Vienna bookshop – one had to climb a narrow spiral staircase to get to it – there was a secret section reserved for a privileged few.' She gave a rare self-satisfied smile. 'I was among them.'

'What was in this secret section?' I asked, emptying the last drop of Alsace wine into her beaker.

'Antiquarian books...books of an esoteric nature, cabalistic, ...books on art, alchemy, on culture...spirituality; astrology and astronomy; renaissance maps of the planets and the stars... they lined the walls all the way up to the ceiling...each one perfectly bound...'

'And Lany? Is he still alive?'

'I often wonder, even now,' she continued, ignoring my question, 'where those magnificent tomes are today...'

The electricity came back on. Adunni stood up and walked around the room snuffing out the candles.

'Lany was arrested and sent to a concentration camp.' She turned her face away but could not hide the anguish in her voice. 'He was beaten to death with a shovel for stealing a potato...'

The plethora of images this brief exchange had summoned up – from Kokoschka to cabalistic books to concentration camps – left us speechless. But the silence spoke. It created an invisible bond. My respect for Adunni increased tenfold.

Later that evening I recalled a snippet of information I'd been given when researching her life ten years earlier. I'd dismissed it at the time as a false rumour. I was eager to interview Ulli Beier about Adunni and her work, but I had no idea of his whereabouts. An acquaintance put me in touch with a Polish friend of his, a collector of African art, who lived in London. When I rang the collector he told me that Ulli was now living in Australia, and gave me his phone number there. Ulli was friendly when I eventually managed to get hold of him, but was adamant that his former wife was a subject he never discussed.

Aware of my own interest in African art, however, the Polish collector later invited me to view his collection of Yoruba *ibeji*. The Yoruba believe that twins share a soul, and when one twin dies the other is given a special consecrated doll, known as an *ibeji*, to carry around. If the second twin dies, another doll is consecrated to match the first, and both are kept by the mother. A matching pair of *ibeji* is a valuable collector's item.

After showing me around his vast *ibeji* collection – many of which were ancient – the collector recounted how Ulli had once told him that Suzanne, as she was known then, had spent time in a concentration camp. There were many unfounded rumours about her circling around, and as she wasn't Jewish, I paid little heed to what he'd told me. But now, knowing that a concentration camp was where captured Resistance operatives, who weren't shot, ended up, I wasn't so sure.

But I understood why, if it was true, she didn't ever speak about it. Adunni would have resented the imputed victimhood, the prurience and the pity. She wanted to be recognised as an artist and as a high priestess of Oshun, not as a concentration camp survivor.

He must have got wind from the owner of the guest house that we were planning to leave. At 7am the following morning our erstwhile stalker banged on the door of our room and demanded to see our passports. Now wearing a frayed police uniform, he was accompanied by a fellow officer in a smarter one. They proceeded to question us about why we were in Oshogbo – so far so ridiculously obvious. The heart-stopping moment came when they informed us they would have to take the passports to the police station to make photocopies. We asked if we could accompany them – once we'd changed out of our pyjamas – but they said the station was 'out of bounds'.

We were at the reception desk attempting to get a line to the British Embassy when they sauntered back in, an hour later.

'Thank you, ladies,' the smarter one grinned as he handed us back our passports. 'That will be all.'

We stayed on in Oshogbo and paid a visit to the artist and expert wood carver, Kasali, one of Adunni's team of New Sacred Artists. And it was outside his wooden shack that I acquired my very own carving of Oshun.

When she eventually landed on my doorstep in Brighton, I wasn't sure whether the goddess should remain in the battered suitcase which had been her home for seventeen days. Apart from having an aversion to travel show-offs who transform their homes into ethnology museums, I didn't know how my new husband would react. My last African acquisition – a white-faced female Ekpe mask with a child's head attached to it – had ended up in the loft. One night David had caught a glimpse of its luminescent visage reflected in the mirror of our darkened hallway and insisted it was too spooky to be on display. I accused him of being scared of a piece of wood.

We had a row.

'That thing's got a weird energy about it,' he had said. 'Take your pick. It's either going in the loft or on the fire.'

Not wanting another African artefacts argument, David agreed that this one wouldn't be consigned to the loft. He even admitted to being a tad beguiled by the near-naked goddess.

'Hardly surprising,' I responded. 'She is, after all, the goddess of female creativity, beauty, sexuality and love…and…and…'

'What?'

'She's also reputed to look at herself in the mirror a lot and have a filthy temper.'

'Sounds just like you.'

'Thanks.'

And when the package arrived from Lagos containing Sally's watercolour, *Mammy Water Visits Brighton*, we decided to hang it on the wall above the goddess's head.

Things Fall Apart

ON A DRIZZLY afternoon, almost a year later, Sally and I stood on Brighton beach, watching a murmuration of starlings swoop over what was left of the West Pier. She'd recently flown back to England under the pretext of visiting family – but with the intention of never returning to Nigeria. Saying little, we continued to trudge across sodden pebbles and slippery seaweed.

Sally wasn't in great shape – physically or emotionally. Since my last visit to Nigeria, undercover police on the lookout for subversive human rights messages had continued to stalk her and her partner's performance troupe, Iwana Arts. The entire troupe had once been arrested. But it was another ordeal Sally wasn't ready to talk about, which had shaken her to the core and led to her decision to quit both the country and her marriage for good.

I was feeling pretty down, too. The production company had been keen to go ahead with the documentary, but wanted to use a particular director who insisted on writing his own narration.

They offered to retain me as a consultant – whatever that meant. Not only had I intended to write the script myself, I was also so uncomfortable with the angle the director was proposing to take that I felt compelled to withdraw the project. I wasn't prepared to betray Adunni's trust. But as we schlepped along the beach that afternoon I was far more concerned about my sister. After almost seven years in Africa, all she'd returned with – to avoid suspicion that she wasn't coming back – was a small suitcase.

Sally had only recently heard the news that her close friend, the singer, Fran Kuboye, had passed away – only a few days after her uncle, the controversial musician and activist, Fela Kuti.

'They're saying he took her with him,' she sighed. 'There is a belief among some Nigerians that the dead can summon a family member to keep them company.'

Nigeria suddenly felt all about endings. We stood on the shore attempting to skim pebbles across the water.

'What I found truly terrifying,' Sally said, breaking the silence, 'is the way the police and armed forces over there are given a free hand to do whatever they want.'

I took her arm. 'Let's get out of the rain.' We wandered over to a small café near the front and propped ourselves on stools in the corner. The waitress came over, and we ordered tea and a plate of chips to share. My sister was finally ready to talk.

'It happened on a Friday evening. Udo and I had arranged to meet a couple of friends from the British Council…'

'Where? In Lagos?'

'Yes, in a bar we hadn't visited before. We drove about for ages, but we couldn't find it. No one was around to ask… Then we spotted this soldier in a dark side alley… We stopped and asked him for directions.'

Her hand began to tremble as she stirred her tea.

'Up close, we could see he had a Kalashnikov slung over his

shoulder and his eyes were red from smoking ganja. He began to interrogate us – ferociously – for no apparent reason other than that he was stoned and bored.'

Sally went on to describe how Udo, objecting to the soldier's rude questioning, became angry and argumentative. The next thing they knew the Kalashnikov was pointed at their heads and they were ordered to drive to the army barracks.

The waitress placed the plate of chips and a bottle of tomato ketchup on the bench in front of us. Neither of us had the appetite for them any more.

'Back at the barracks,' Sally continued in a hushed voice, 'I was accused of being a spy and warned that it carried the death penalty.'

'Bloody hell, Sally, that's terrifying...'

'An army clerk sat at a desk typing out a statement which I was ordered to sign.' She pushed the chips around the plate with her fork.

'When I refused to sign it we were forced to the floor with guns pointing at us and ordered to beg for our lives.'

Tears welled up in her eyes. I put my hand on hers. A swarm of rowdy French school kids piled into the café, taking up every remaining table.

'Do you want to go?'

Sally nodded.

We continued our walk along the front. It wasn't until we reached Brighton Palace Pier that she felt ready to resume her story.

'The cell they locked us up in had fresh blood on the walls... I was so terrified I couldn't swallow; Udo went to pieces... became a helpless heap on the cell floor. I had no idea what was going to happen...'

The rain was now lashing down. We took shelter on the pier.

A handful of day trippers in anoraks and waterproofs were braving the few rides which were in operation. Not that long ago, one gloriously sunny day when they were over for my wedding, Sally and Udo had shrieked with excited laughter as they clung on to the bars of the Waltzer.

As difficult as it was for Sally to continue her story, my imagination was now running riot; I was anxious for her to get to the end.

'What happened next? Please carry on. You were in the cell…?'

'OK. I suddenly visualised Mum at home, knitting by the fire. What the hell am I doing here? I asked myself… Somehow I found the strength to start chanting… Then I got really angry…'

'I guess you'd been so overwhelmed with fear…'

'Yeah. I hadn't dared to allow myself to feel rage until then. My life is too big for this I thought. I refuse to die in this shit-hole.'

Sally started to cry properly. We turned our backs on the rides and gazed out at the waves crashing into the pier.

'…I felt like Alice in Wonderland; as if my head and shoulders were breaking out of the cell…'

'Wow.'

'A short time after that a guard unlocked the door and slung us out. We were thrown into our car at gunpoint and ordered to drive. One of the soldiers warned us that we'd have our brains blown out if we looked back.'

The trauma of that episode proved to be the final straw for Sally. She felt unprotected; her partner no longer seemed able to control either his temper or his drinking; nor did he appreciate the threat both posed to their personal safety.

Sally sighed, pensively. 'I learnt so much more about life through being married to someone from a different culture. I still care about him, but…'

'*Things Fall Apart*,' I piped up, quoting the title of a book by the acclaimed Nigerian author, Chinua Achebe. 'I think living in a chaotic country like Nigeria puts additional pressures on a relationship – especially if you're a foreigner. Adunni didn't manage to sustain hers.'

I took her arm. 'Come on, you're safe now, let's go home.'

A year later, General Sani Abacha, the corrupt and ruthless de facto President of Nigeria, died of a Viagra-induced heart attack while entertaining two Indian prostitutes in the presidential villa in Abuja. No doubt about it, he and a few of those other post-colonial rulers would have given the Borgias a good run for their money.

General Obasanjo, Sally's friend and former boss, was released from prison and the following year, 1999, he was elected Head of State once again. In his eight years in office he not only restored democracy, he managed to recover US$770 million of stolen state cash, mounted a purge on corruption in all public offices and became a champion of conflict resolution on the African continent.

Parallel Lives

I MAY HAVE given up on the idea of a documentary, but Adunni's life and work continued to inspire me. Nor had I lost my desire to share the beauty and complexity of Ifa and the *orisha* with a wider audience; the African art, culture and indigenous religion she championed played too small a part on the world stage. I applied to the Arts Council for a grant to write a stage play with an African theme.

While awaiting their response I began to research the life and work of other western artists for whom Africa had been a powerful source of inspiration. One, in particular, leapt out at me.

In my late teens I'd purchased a humongous poster, Blu-tacked it to the wall, and placed an African rubber plant beside it. Superimposed onto an all-white background, the poster depicted the beaded head and shoulders of a spear-holding, imaginatively-tattooed, stunningly handsome African tribesman. On the poster there was no indication of where the picture had been taken, or who had taken it. During my exploration of Africa-influenced western artists, I came across a copy of the original photograph; it had been shot in the Sudan by Hitler's favourite filmmaker, Leni Riefenstahl.

I was fascinated to discover, besides physical beauty and a Germanic background, how much Suzanne Wenger and Leni Riefenstahl had in common. Riefenstahl, too, had made the journey to Africa in the early 1950s, and had come under the continent's spell. Highly respected in their respective fields of art and film, both women had also shared the misfortune of being caught up in the malignant maelstrom of the Third Reich.

Beginning her career as a much-fêted dancer, Leni went on to become a celebrated film actress. For the sake of cinematic art she climbed mountains, icebergs, glaciers, sat buried in snow for hours and was once hauled along an ice wall as avalanches plunged over her. Not content with being a mere actress she then went on to direct movies. Whatever your political persuasion, from an artistic perspective her epic documentaries – *Triumph of the Will*, depicting the 1934 Nuremberg Rally, and *Olympia*, the 1936 Berlin Olympic Games, are cinematographic masterpieces. Unfortunately, *Triumph of the Will* also remains the magnum opus of Nazi propaganda. It comes as no surprise that she received film offers from Stalin and Mussolini.

While Suzanne Wenger and her artist-friend who had deserted from the front stood at her studio window and watched as Nazi soldiers marched into Vienna, Leni Riefenstahl was sitting on a train bound for Innsbruck. The Ministry of Propaganda had informed the director that the release of *Olympia*, the film she'd laboured over for years, was to be delayed indefinitely because Austria had just been annexed to the Third Reich. She tracked Hitler down to his Innsbruck hotel and was granted an audience. 'How delighted I am that you can witness this great moment,' he told her. Capitalising on Hitler's elevated mood, she impulsively suggested that his birthday – 20th April – would be a good date to release *Olympia*. To her delight he agreed, and gave orders for a grand reception to be held afterwards, at which she would be the guest of honour. Meanwhile, Suzanne's deserter friend painted his beautiful picture, gave himself up and was shot. While Leni continued to hobnob with Hitler, Suzanne joined the Austrian Resistance.

Leni Riefenstahl paid a high price for her association with her Führer. Even though she hadn't been a member of the Nazi Party, she was vilified after the war. Despite her insistence that she'd disapproved of Hitler's persecution of the Jews and hadn't been aware of the existence of concentration camps, she was accused of using gypsies from a camp as film slaves. A woman personally testified that she'd seen several of these gypsy extras being gassed at Auschwitz; an accusation which Leni vigorously denied. All her property was confiscated and her livelihood destroyed.

She was officially cleared by the Denazification Tribunal, but there is no denying the fact that Leni Riefenstahl's extraordinary talent had helped to bolster Hitler's monstrous regime. Leni was more driven by her art than by her conscience; Suzanne more by her conscience than her art.

Their reasons for decamping to Africa may appear, on the surface, to be those of cultural curiosity or the search for artistic inspiration – and in the case of Suzanne, love – but it could also have been a desire to escape the psychological and emotional toxicity of stigma. While I have no reason to disbelieve the Polish collector's assertion that Suzanne spent time in a concentration camp, it's still hearsay. But there is no doubting the fact that Leni spent three years in camps and prisons and four months in an insane asylum.

Parallels persisted, too, around their arrivals in Africa. Suzanne almost died of tuberculosis soon after she arrived and Leni nearly lost her life in a car crash north of Nairobi when her upper torso smashed through the windscreen. When the pilot arrived to fly her to the hospital he told the driver he was wasting his money as she'd never make it there alive. But survive, she did. And it was while glancing at a magazine in the hospital that she caught her first glimpse of the Nuba of the Sudan. The image she found so arresting was of a wrestler, caked in ash, being carried on the shoulders of a friend. His body, she reflected, was like a sculpture by Michelangelo or Rodin. And so began a new phase of her career: photography.

Leni's fascination with the Nuba extended beyond the purely artistic; it amounted to love. She described them as the happiest people on earth, who laughed all time. And the Nuba, it would seem, loved the childless, friendless Leni. Just as Suzanne had found love and acceptance with the ancient priests and priestesses she'd chanced upon in Ede, so the Nuba took Leni to their hearts. She decided to live among them. They built her a small straw hut and brought her presents of calabashes, spears, jewellery and musical instruments. She later claimed she was the happiest she'd ever been in her life. But her love affair with the Nuba wasn't destined to end well.

Photographs of the mesmerisingly attractive tribespeople and their extraordinary, Picasso-like body-paint designs won Leni a gold medal from the Art Directors Club of Germany, Sudanese citizenship – courtesy of the President – and worldwide praise, but they also earned her damning criticism. Her pictures of the Nuba, some believed, reflected her fascist longings. One German critic wrote: '*In her latest work she has found her way from the black corps of the SS to the black bodies of the Nuba...there is a lingering desire for black SS uniforms. A continuing fascination with the body beautiful.'*

Suzanne, too, was presented with a gold medal by the Austrian government for her artistic achievements, and the Nigerian president signed a decree preserving the shrines, but although Leni's critics were crueller, Suzanne also came in for a lot of flak. She was accused of plundering a valuable ethnic resource for the sake of her art, and her work was unfairly criticised as being a European projection; a falsification of African culture.

While Suzanne believed the ancient culture of Ifa was being denied its importance and relevance to global culture – thereby continuing the colonial strategy of incapacitation – Leni also felt the world had much to learn from the kindness, generosity, simplicity, meaningful rituals and lifestyle of the talented Nuba. In the face of the harsh criticisms and accusations both women suffered, it isn't difficult to understand why Leni sought refuge in her Nuba family, and Suzanne in her grateful goddess, Oshun.

In exchange for taking their photographs, Leni had only ever given the Nuba medicine and oil. But, sadly, the popularity of her images attracted tourists, who traded money, alcohol and cigarettes to take pictures of their own. She was shocked, on a later visit there, to be asked by the Nuba for tobacco, clothes, batteries and sunglasses. At the wrestling festivals, the wrestlers, who were once covered only in ash, wore dirty, ragged clothes. Instead of beautifully decorated calabashes, they carried plastic bottles and tin cans. Their innocence had been destroyed.

But she couldn't be held entirely responsible for their exit from Eden. The Islamic government in the Sudan had, in the meantime, built roads into Nubaland and forced these unselfconsciously naked tribespeople into clothes.

In the final analysis, Leni Riefenstahl contributed to the demise of an extraordinary culture, whereas Suzanne Wenger, through fighting to have the Sacred Groves declared a World Heritage Site, was instrumental in preserving one. And when the Arts Council of Great Britain decided to award me a grant to write my Africa play I decided to base it on the lives of these two extraordinary women.

Adiós & Auf Wiedersehen

I NAMED the memorial sculpture I commissioned for my son, Sacha, *El Viajero*. Translated into English it means *The Traveller*. The sculpture has a Spanish name because Sacha was half-Colombian, and had loved travelling in South America. I'd only just finished the Wenger/Riefenstahl play when he passed away in 2005. Two weeks after that, my script agent had to retire due to ill health. Adunni, the play, and much else in my life became buried in grief.

That same year, thanks to Adunni's efforts, the Sacred Groves were declared a World Heritage Site. But my interest in life itself had shrivelled up – and that included the continent where it supposedly began. Desperate to remain close to anyone, anything or anywhere connected to my son, my focus had shifted to Latin America. I had, by this time, qualified as a psychotherapist. When I wasn't seeing clients, I worked on my book about Sacha's life and my solo journey to Peru to scatter his ashes.

El Viajero was erected in the winter of 2009/10 at the top of my hillside garden in Surrey. Abnormally cold by British standards, the media called it 'The Big Freeze.' Sleet was starting to thaw the frozen snow at the top of the garden when my son's best friend, Phil, a sculptor, arrived with his young apprentice, a lad called Alfie, to put up the sculpture; a wrought iron structure that he'd laboured over, on and off, for a couple of years.

I'd made up my mind that the completion of the sculpture would be a moving-on point for me; an opportunity to fully embrace life once again. Craving sunshine and warmth, I'd decided, a few days earlier, that I'd brave the Oshun festival, visit Adunni and finally take part in one or two of the goddess's rituals.

Adunni, in the meantime, had become something of an unwilling celebrity. Nigeria was proud that it now had its own World Heritage Site. Credited with being instrumental in helping to revive Ifa in Nigeria, and hence its cultural heritage, she had had a Nigerian street named after her, and her achievements were now included in the national school curriculum. Although I hadn't been in touch with the high priestess for a number of years, there were so many questions I wanted to ask her, still, and matters I wanted to discuss – including my loss. This woman had managed to survive so many bitter challenges in her life, I was hoping she might offer me a few tips on how to keep going.

But very little in my life ever goes according to plan. When I went online to research the dates for the Oshun festival I chanced upon Adunni's obituary in the *Guardian*.

And I was devastated.

I learnt she'd died, earlier that year, in the Oshogbo hospital she'd been admitted to the evening before. Adunni had, apparently, taken a leisurely bath and afterwards had drunk a cup of tea. Surrounded by her extended family, she asked them which day of the week it was, and the time. They told her, and she responded with a smile.

'Ah, so it is time to go. It is good. It is OK.' And with those words she breathed her last and promptly died. She was buried that same evening.

Two weeks prior to her death, Adunni had been awarded what was considered, in Nigeria, to be a great national honour. President Umaru Yar'Adua had made her a Member of the Federal Republic.

Acknowledging her contribution to the country, the Governor of Oshun State, Olagunsoye Oyinlola, described her death as the end of an era in the cultural world, and spoke of her remarkable devotion to the worship of Oshun. 'The late artist,' Oyinlola claimed, 'represented a bridge across continents and across cultures. She came from Western Europe in the early 1950s in search of her *ori inu* (her real essence), which she later discovered in the bosom of the spirituality of Oshun.' Her life, he said, 'was a lesson in being true to oneself and to whatever one is committed to.'

OK, so she was 93, and what a life she'd led. But I'd so wanted to meet her again. I kicked myself for not having got my act together sooner. I'd been intending, for some time, to let her know that the following March, the British museum would be opening a major exhibition of art and sculpture from the ancient kingdom of Ilé-Ifè, the birthplace of the *orisha*; the very same works of art that Adunni had discussed with me years earlier. The British Museum intended to display the Ilé-Ifè sculptures alongside an exhibition of Italian Renaissance drawings in order to make the point that at exactly the same time in West Africa, art of the same level and the same quality was being produced. She would have loved that.

I read her obituary over and over again. And I wept.

Even if I did make the trip to Oshogbo I wouldn't be able

to visit her grave. To discourage tomb worshippers and tourists, she left instructions that she should be laid to rest in one of the sacred shrines and that her whereabouts should remain secret. I couldn't face going to the Sacred Groves without Adunni being there. African sunshine now seemed a distant dream.

Needless to say, I was already feeling pretty emotional when Phil and Alfie arrived to put up Sacha's memorial sculpture. It took them all day to erect *El Viajero* because the sleet had turned to rain and the concrete refused to set. I stood at the top of my garden under a big umbrella, holding the torch as Phil finished off the final bits of welding in semi-darkness.

Afterwards, we went indoors and drank a few beers together while we warmed ourselves by the fire. Alfie and his mother had just got back from the Gambia. He went on and on about what a wonderful holiday they'd had. I looked up fares – it was cheap to fly there – much cheaper than to Nigeria. As soon as they left I booked flights for David and myself.

My spirits lifted the moment I stepped off the plane and felt the African sun on my face. But my enthusiasm was short-lived. The Gambia was a tourist mecca awash with young men who give up on their dreams and end up as the bumster toy boys of western grannies – a gender reversal of what has, for years, been going on in Thailand.

Following in the footsteps of a few of Nigeria's corrupt leaders, Yahya Jammeh, the narcissistic president, had managed to earn himself the nickname: *the worst dictator you've never heard of*. Believed by many to be insane, the idiot claimed to have invented a miracle cure for Aids. His 'cure', which consisted of a mixture of herbal medicine, spiritual healing techniques and the recitation of verses from the Koran, only 'worked' on Thursdays and Mondays. Anti-retroviral drugs were forbidden. Countless people died.

Inland, we were disturbed to see the ominous proliferation of lavish, Saudi-built, Wahhabi mosques peppering the landscape of the most poverty-stricken areas. Gleaming, white-washed semi-citadels with huge golden domes hovered above tiny grass-roofed mud huts where hungry-eyed kids without shoes besieged our Land Rover, begging for pencils and food.

Apart from megalithic stone circles in Wassau and the depressing remnants of the slave trade, the country seemed devoid of much history, or of the archaic culture which had so captivated me in Nigeria. Given that there were Gambians of Yoruba descent in this tiny West African country, I'd hoped to see a few signs of Ifa culture, or even a shrine to the odd *orisha* or two, but there was nothing. The religion and culture were heavily patriarchal. Gambian women appeared submissive. This was truly a goddess-forsaken land.

I wondered whether my love affair with Africa was finally over.

Part 2

America:
The Sacred Orisha
Gardens

Dark Matter

ALL THAT IS visible – the Earth, the sun, the stars and galaxies – only make up five per cent of our universe. The remainder consists of mysterious, invisible elements which perplexed scientists have named dark energy and dark matter. *Orisha*, too, are mysterious, invisible elements. I was keen to gain a better understanding of the 'dark' energy of Oshun, the *orisha* who had 'touched' me in her sacred river all those years ago. But I knew I couldn't properly comprehend her energy unless I truly opened myself to experiencing the power of Ifa through engaging in rituals. I was toying, once again, with the idea of attending the Oshun Festival.

I had, at this point in my life, been living and working in Salford Quays, Manchester for four years. In 2012, the television programme David works on was relocated up north and I decided to come with him. Life in culture-dense MediaCity certainly had its vibrant ups – but also its definite downs; apart from the tiny Blue Peter Garden, it was a concrete jungle; then there was the question of the weather. The Quays had its own micro-climate: a windy, wet one.

A new client turning up in my psychotherapy clinic is what triggered my renewed interest in delving, yet again, into the *orisha*. This client not only compounded my stress levels but also caused me to reflect on my own assumptions and biases where inexplicable phenomena are concerned. The client in question was a young Pakistani woman who was convinced she was possessed by a *jinn*.

Jinns are supernatural entities mentioned regularly in the Qu'ran; they can be neutral, or good, or evil. This one, the young woman assured me, was definitely evil. She'd been told as much by 'an expert' who was also an Imam, and who wished to conduct an exorcism. Before she underwent the exorcism she wanted to see if counselling would help. Her work provided private health cover and the exorcism was, apparently, expensive. I was perturbed: the young woman in question had a degree in psychology.

I spent a couple of hours getting myself spooked-out watching *jinn* exorcisms on YouTube. A poor man who was thrashing around on the floor of a mosque, and was cited as 'proof' of the existence of *jinn*, was quite clearly having an epileptic fit. The creepy voices coming from *jinn*-possessed clients on exorcists' couches struck me more as evidence of dissociative personality disorder – where one or more additional personalities exist in one individual – than possession.

My client's history and my professional head told me she was clinically depressed, yet another part of me was asking why it was that I defaulted immediately to a 'medical' position while at the same time being prepared to believe in the existence of these *orisha* who also, from time to time, 'possessed' their followers.

According to Jung, possession has by no means become

obsolete – only the name has changed; the psychic conditions which bred demons, are, he believes, as actively at work as ever. The demons have not really disappeared but have merely taken on another form: they have become unconscious psychic forces.

This left me wondering whether the *orisha*, too, were unconscious psychic forces. I once touched on the subject with Adunni. 'But do the *orisha* exist inside or outside of us, Adunni?'

I remember her giving me a rare smile. 'That, my dear, is something you would need to discover for yourself.'

I opened the blinds and watched as rain poured out of Lowry-grey skies. Yet another Sunday when it was too wet to walk. Ernest Hemingway's words leapt into head: *I never knew of a morning in Africa when I woke up and was not happy*. I glanced over at my Oshun. She was staring out of the window onto the sepia waters of Salford Quays. And she looked bloody miserable, too.

Once the rain had subsided I grabbed my coat and dashed out. Despite the plastic bags, punctured bike tyres and unidentifiable detritus floating alongside me, I was managing to enjoy a brisk walk alongside the Manchester Ship Canal, until I found myself having to weave my way through scores of chanting blue and red City and United fans, jostling their way to Old Trafford for the local derby. Clutching cans of Fosters to their tattooed torsos like weapons, they reminded me of rowdy tribal gatherings I'd seen in Africa, which, like this crowd, looked ferocious at first glance, but were usually pretty friendly.

The sun decided to make a brief appearance. Wishing to make the most of this rare occurrence I managed to locate a canal-side bench that wasn't covered in seagull crap. Undeterred by the roars and chants echoing from the stadium, a bedraggled-looking fox attempted to extract the remnants of a Big Mac from the carton a supporter had chucked beside the canal. I shut my eyes and deliberately recalled the tranquil, aquatic environs of the Sacred Groves, and the time when Sally and I had stripped down to our underwear and bathed together in Oshun's river. Apart from birdsong and the gentle lapping of the water, silence had reigned. We had luxuriated in the beauty, peace and solitude surrounding us. The river seemed to bring us closer as sisters.

I opened my eyes and on an impulse took my phone from my pocket and called Sally. These days, my sister was living close to the sea in Essex, with the two children the priest and priestess had predicted she would have when they read her cowrie shells in the Sacred Groves all those years ago. What they hadn't told her about the children (now teenagers) was that they would be twins – so special and beloved by the Yoruba. Sally had given birth to my nephew and niece a couple of years after moving back to England, and viewed them as a 'gift' from Africa for her time and efforts there. She was no longer with the twins' father, but was thriving happily as an artist and a teacher of art.

Sally was on her way out and told me to make it quick.

'Are you up for a trip to Nigeria, Sally?

A long silence followed. I tried again.

'How about coming to the Oshun festival with me this year? I feel I owe it to Adunni to connect properly with Oshun. I told her I'd take part in rituals one day...'

I could hear her thinking. In the intervening years I'd been back to Nigeria only once. She hadn't been there at all.

'I'm not sure Di... I'm not sure... I'd certainly love to visit the Sacred Groves again...'

Then, to my delight, she burst into excited chatter about all the friends she could catch up with and the sketches she could make of the festival.

'I need to sleep on it. I'll get back to you... Sorry, I really must dash...'

Storm clouds appeared out of nowhere. Hail began to fall. I jogged home feeling hopeful.

A few days later Sally called me to say she'd been waking up in the night having Nigeria-related anxiety attacks. She didn't feel ready to go back. While I understood, I couldn't pretend not to be disappointed.

I was gutted when my Pakistani client quit after only a couple of sessions, telling me she'd decided to go ahead with the exorcism because 'counselling wasn't working'. But her departure made me even more determined to find out the truth of *orisha* for myself.

Shango

A FEW DAYS later I switched on the radio and received a brutal reminder of the side to sub-Saharan Africa that Hemingway on his big game safaris didn't get to see, but his fellow author, Joseph Conrad, did. The last words uttered by Conrad's character, Kurtz, in the author's novel *Heart of Darkness*, based upon his own experiences in the Congo Free State, were *The horror! The horror!*

Listening to the news report it seemed that Shango, the *orisha* of thunder, lightning and war, was on the rampage once again in West Africa. Boko Haram, which had taken over from Isis as the world's most deadly terrorist organisation, was on a killing spree. This radical Islamist sect had murdered more people than Isis, to whom they had recently sworn allegiance. Now they wanted to be known as Iswap – Islamic State West African Province.

Fundamentalism is a curse to be found in all religions. Years ago, when I taught English at the Muslim College in London, I came to understand that Islam is, first and foremost, a peace-loving faith. My students, male and female, were a mixture of Sunni and Shia. From Africa, India, Pakistan, Iran, Iraq and Malaysia, they all mixed happily together. A few would come along with me to Buddhist meetings; the discussions were lively and the atmosphere warm and friendly. My heart went out to those Muslims who were being tarred with the same fundamentalist brush.

Two young female suicide bombers, the reporter said, had blown themselves up in Dikwa refugee camp for internally displaced people in Maiduguri, the north-eastern birthplace of this Nigerian insurgency, which had wormed its way into Cameroon, Chad and Niger. Some believed the insurgency, which had seen 20,000 lives lost and 2.3 million West Africans displaced, was funded by members of a Nigerian elite who wanted to establish a Sharia state.

The young women had killed at least sixty of the refugees. But some were spared when a third intended bomber realised, at the last minute, that her family had taken shelter there too, and refused to detonate her explosives. I felt my heart slowly sink. Only ten days ago eighty-six people lost their lives when another two female bombers blew themselves up. These young female suicide bombers were also suspected to be a radicalised contingent of the 219 Christian schoolgirls who were abducted from their secondary school in the town of Chibok in Borno State, Nigeria, by Boko Haram fighters in April 2014, prompting the global *Bring Back Our Girls* campaign.

No wonder my Oshun looked so miserable. Shango, the god of war, was brutalising and killing her beloved daughters, and to make matters worse the poor goddess was married to him.

I wondered whether going on my own to Nigeria in this incendiary climate was really such a good idea. David had already declined my invitation to accompany me. I decided to launch a second cajoling attack but made the mistake of relating Sally's reasons for not wanting to go.

'And what about *your* personal safety?'

'I know I haven't been back for a few years, but I can look after myself. I've been going there since I was twenty-four. I know my way around.'

'Hmm.'

'If you're so worried, why don't you come with me?'

'Look what happened in Ouagadougou, the capital of Burkina Faso, last month. It's virtually next door to Nigeria.'

'What happened?'

An Al-Qaeda cell killed more than thirty people in a hotel and coffee bar. They shot aid workers, tourists and a missionary.'

'It's happening everywhere these days,' I told him. 'We can't let them stop us travelling.'

'Yeah, well you might get to change your mind if you see some of the gore I have to edit out of the footage that comes in. *You* only get to see the sanitised version.'

There is definitely a downside to being married to a television news editor.

'Those gunmen were handpicking the people with white faces,' said David, giving me a hug. 'If you want to go, go, but I'd be worried about you. I'm taking the camper van up to Sweden and Norway. You're welcome to come with me.'

I took myself off to Holland for a few days to temporarily satisfy my wanderlust and distract myself from having to decide whether or not I should risk going to the festival. The rain came too. Under an umbrella, I admired the wonderful collection of wildlife in Artis, Amsterdam's Royal Zoo – and one of the oldest in Europe.

With me was my Dutch friend, Harriet. We let ourselves into the zoo. Harriet had her own key, which I found really exciting in a childish sort of way. She'd become quite big in the sustainability movement and had recently been appointed Head of Education at the zoo. We met years ago in New York and have been close ever since. A very tall, attractive blonde, and clever with it, Harriet exuded strength but was quite fragile following her recent divorce.

We took a look at Harriet's favourite zoo inhabitants – the penguins. She explained that quite a few of them were gay and mated for life; they'd become champions of gay rights in Holland. The lucky ones were given their own egg to hatch and they made great parents. The zoo offered special tours to educate the public about the prevalence of homosexual behaviour in the wildlife kingdom – from gorillas to vultures.

'That wouldn't go down too well in Africa,' I remarked. 'It's illegal in thirty-four African countries and punishable by death in northern Nigeria.'

Harriet sighed heavily. A sign she was getting fed up with me flip-flopping around over Nigeria.

'That's no reason not to go! You've been there enough times, and to other far-flung places on your own: Southeast Asia, India, Egypt, Peru... Are you losing your nerve, Diane?' she asked, impatiently.

'Yes.'

'Come on, you need cheering up.' She tugged at my sleeve. 'First of all I'm going to show you our baby gorilla – he's only a week old. Then we're going to the Buddhist centre.'

It was my turn to sigh. I pulled up my hood, eased my bum onto the back of Harriet's dripping-wet push bike and we splashed down the cycle lanes all the way to Van Kinsbergenstraat.

As if on cue, when the chanting ended an elderly Japanese gentleman hobbled to his feet and read out encouraging statistics about the ever-increasing number of Africans who were now practising our type of socially inclusive Buddhism. Harriet, whom I introduced to the practice years ago, smiled at me. I felt a smidgen of hope where gay and religious persecution issues in Africa were concerned. I also decided to get in touch with my good friend Boye. After all, his mother was the *Aare Iyalode* of Oshogbo – the second-in-command to the head of all the women in Oshogboland.

Boye was delighted when I told him that I might be over soon for the Oshun Festival. Resisting lucrative offers of work from abroad, (unlike so many African professionals), he'd chosen, instead, to remain in Africa, where his talents were most needed. Since I'd last seen him he'd been working with The World Health Organisation rolling out malaria programmes all over Africa, while continuing to conduct research into the medicinal properties of African plants. He'd also set up his own NGO, which trains doctors and nurses and conducts research into childhood illnesses and malnutrition. The NGO also helps to educate girls who are at risk of being exploited for child labour or sex; one in the eye for Boko Haram.

Boye's enthusiasm around my proposed visit clinched it; I was definitely going. He offered to arrange meetings in Oshogbo with experts in both the cultural and spiritual aspects of Oshun worship.

There was an elephant in our living room. And it was definitely an African, not an Asian elephant. I visited my parents and discovered they had one in theirs too. It made its presence known when I was on the point of leaving.

Not only did my parents not understand why I didn't want to drive thousands of miles across Europe and Scandinavia with my petrol-head partner to fulfil his long-held ambition of playing a round of golf on the most northerly golf course in the world, they couldn't comprehend why I could possibly want to go back to Nigeria.

'Isn't your Buddhism enough for you? my father asked. 'Why, in heaven's name, do you need to start messing around with African gods? And anyway, what's wrong with Sweden and Norway?'

'I'd go bonkers being cooped up in the van, Dad. He's planning to cover hundreds of miles a day. One of our bodies would end up in the fjords.'

'I'd rather see the Northern Lights,' my mother piped up, 'than get mixed up in all that *juju* business.'

'Don't worry, Mum,' I lied. 'I won't be getting into any of that.'

All I needed now was the date of the Oshun festival so that I could book my flight. While searching online for this elusive date I came across a notification that Oshun rituals would be taking place in The Sacred Orisha Gardens which were part of The Ifa Foundation. This confused me. I read on and discovered that these sacred gardens weren't in Nigeria, at all, but in Florida. I was still unable to ascertain the date of the Oshun festival, but my curiosity was aroused.

La Paloma Blanca

THE FOREIGN Office put the lid on my proposed trip to Nigeria. Following a spate of Boko Haram atrocities, a warning was suddenly issued against travelling in or near the north of Nigeria, or attending religious ceremonies and festivals anywhere in the country. To go to the festival in spite of this warning would mean no travel insurance cover and stressed-out loved-ones.

Disappointed that I would miss the festival, I had another look at the Ifa Foundation in Florida. A certain Professor Robin Poynor of the University of Florida described it as having *the only complete sacred orisha garden in the Western Hemisphere*. The foundation apparently attracted worshippers from all over the world. A section of its website was in Spanish and there was a good smattering of black and Hispanic-looking people taking part in their rituals. Many came in from the islands around Florida – including Cuba. I suspected their ancestors had been part of the Yoruba diaspora. As my sole exposure to Ifa had been in West Africa, I was curious to learn more about where it was practised in other parts of the world, and how the belief system had diversified following the diaspora.

Ifa, I learnt, was transported from West Africa via the Atlantic slave trade to other parts of the world during the four centuries of The Middle Passage. *Orisha* worship proliferated under an assortment of labels in these various terrains, including Regla de Ocha, Lucumí and Santería in Cuba, North America and the Spanish Caribbean, and Candomblé in Brazil. *Orisha* communities also settled in parts of Europe and Asia – indeed, wherever slaves, former slaves or their ancestors had established roots. The gods and goddesses, too, were given different names. Ochún and Oxúm are just a couple of Oshun's diasporic aliases, along with Mami Wata (the pidgin pronunciation of Mammy Water).

A number of these variations of Ifa combined the Yoruba deities with Catholic saints. Originally imported by foreign conquerors such as the Spanish and the Portuguese, these saints were imposed on the indigenous inhabitants of those countries, and later on the slaves transported from West Africa. By combining *orisha* with Catholic saints, the slaves managed to fool unsuspecting slave masters and practise the religion of their ancestors beneath the veneer of Christianity. In conflict-prone regions, Shango, the god of war, came to be associated with St Barbara, the patron saint of militiamen. In Cuba, Oshun merged with the patron saint of the country, Our Lady of Charity – an aspect of the Virgin Mary that related to hope and survival. Obatala, the *orisha* of purity, wisdom, justice and the dove sometimes masqueraded as Jesus Christ.

When Fidel Castro entered Havana on 8th January 1959, and delivered his triumphant victory speech to the people of Cuba, a white dove landed on his shoulder and another on the rostrum, and stayed there for his two-hour oration (a relatively short one for this notoriously verbose leader). *La Paloma Blanca* was dismissed by some of the international media as a mere coincidence, and hailed by others as a token of peace. But for the Lucumí and Santería worshippers who had been making consistent sacrifices to the *orisha* in support of Fidel, and had fought alongside him against the ruthless, US-backed, right-wing dictator, Fulgencio Batista, the doves were a symbol of divine approval. Fidel was their liberator; the *orisha's* chosen one. Castro, in turn, embraced the Afro-Cuban community; the descendents of slaves.

Over the centuries, more than a million West Africans had been shipped to the small island to labour on its sugar cane and tobacco plantations. A slave master who had been excessively cruel would sometimes find a dead dove on his doorstep as a warning to mend his ways, or else...

I used to think the Havana dove spectacle had been stage-managed until I looked at some original footage on YouTube. Castro delivers his speech outdoors; there are thousands of people in the crowd. A dove is squatting on *his* shoulder – no one else's. I'm sure that during his final guerrilla offensive and gruelling march on Havana he wouldn't have had much time to spare for dove-training. The footage made me shiver.

Orisha have also managed to infiltrate national customs and celebrations. Over the New Year, millions of Brazilians float candles and throw flowers, perfume and food into the sea for Yemoja – the *orisha* of the oceans (considered, by some, to be the salt-water aspect of Oshun). Not all of those on Copacabana beach and other shorelines who make offerings to the goddess in the hope that she will grant good fortune for the year ahead are Candomblé practitioners. Thousands upon thousands of Brazilians have simply embraced the activity as a national tradition.

I was intrigued to learn more about how Ifa was currently being practised in The United States. After deliberating for a week or so I decided to send the Ifa Foundation in Florida a message of enquiry, mentioning that I had known Suzanne Wenger. A couple of days later – on African Heritage Day, 5th May to be precise – I received a reply:

> *Alafia Diane*
>
> *We want to welcome you to the Ifa Foundation…ashe!*
>
> *We have enjoyed sharing the wisdom and knowledge of the path of Ifa…with seekers from around the globe.*
>
> *The experience of meeting Suzanne must have been an incredible moment in your life. I have not physically met her…but have connected for many years and have built a piece in her honor inside the Sacred Orisha Gardens in central Florida.*
>
> *We welcome you to come and experience your rituals inside the sacred gates and feel the incredible transformation present.*
>
> *love and light*
>
> *ashe*
>
> *Iyanifa Vassa*

I arranged a Skype call with this Iyanifa Vassa. I'd been anticipating an ageing hippy, but instead found myself talking with an intelligent, articulate woman who trained as an interior architect and had been involved with the *orisha* for over thirty years.

In the course of our conversation I learnt that Iyanifa (Mother of Divination) Vassa and her partner, Oluwo (Master of Secrets) Philip, were also white initiates. Before they became acquainted with the Yoruba tradition of Ifa, they'd practised its diasporic offshoot, Santería. In the years that followed they'd been attempting – not without difficulty – to establish the tradition in North America.

Vassa's assurance that it would be possible for me to participate in non-blood-letting rituals nailed it for me. I agreed I'd come over in the summer and experience, finally, some Ifa rituals for myself. This time Sally jumped at the offer of joining me.

Sculpture Park

THE IRONY wasn't lost on me. The day after booking my flight to 'safe' Florida to avoid the possibility of an attack by Isis-affiliated terrorists in Nigeria, forty-nine people were murdered at a gay nightclub in Orlando by a gunman pledging allegiance to Isis.

Fast on the heels of this came further disconcerting news that a two-year-old boy had been snatched and killed by an alligator in Florida's Disney World; not that I'd intended going there – alligator or no alligator. I decided, however, to pay a visit to the place in England that came closest to being Disney World for me: Yorkshire Sculpture Park. Parts of the park stirred up memories of the Sacred Groves of Oshogbo. I needed, somehow, to connect with Adunni; I was beginning to have second thoughts about Florida.

My Floridian cold feet had more to do with my recent Guardian Orisha Life Path Divination than with Isis or alligators.

I'd always assumed that Oshun was my guardian *orisha*, but, over the years, the more I'd learnt about the agonies and antics of the Yoruba gods and goddesses the less certain I'd become; it was like researching your medical symptoms online and coming away convinced you could have any number of diseases. The Ifa Foundation had a variety of initiations, rituals and healing ceremonies on offer. One that caught my eye was an Orisha Guardian Divination via Skype. Forewarned is forearmed. I wanted this guardian *orisha* business clarified before I left for Florida.

I was about to send Vassa an email requesting the Orisha Guardian Divination when one from her popped into my mailbox:

I want to map out with you what you want to do with the Ifa
Foundation ceremonial-wise.

I know you had spoken about initiation. There are layers of
aligning for that, so with the time coming closer…

Initiation! I started to panic. At no point had I requested or even remotely suggested a priestess initiation. Participating in Ifa rituals would be enough of a challenge. I took a deep breath and in response explained that I didn't feel quite ready for an initiation but that before going to Florida I'd like to have a Guardian Orisha Life Path Divination. Vassa offered to throw in a Guardian Ancestor Divination for nothing.

A few days later the Guardian Orisha Life Path Divination arrived in my mailbox – all seven pages of it. I was relieved to have confirmation that Oshun, was, indeed, my very own guardian *orisha*. But I found the reading itself rather obtuse; it appeared to range from the incomprehensible: *See evolution and elevation working through cooperation and integration.* To the bleedin' obvious: *Don't be a victim. Be a victor!* Perhaps I was missing something.

As it transpired, it served me right for not reading the small print. Vassa explained, in a follow-up Skype call, that it was the reading given to babies when they were three days old; this particular divination was not about my destiny, as such, she said, but about focusing on the *orisha* energies that are uniquely mine to draw on throughout my life; people in their eighties, she assured me, still have this divination.

I asked her how she'd worked out my life path and she explained that she'd used palm nuts and a divining chain known as an *opele*. She flashed her *opele* at the screen and told me that it had been given to her by Suzanne Wenger, via an intermediary, and that she'd used it to divine which *odu* came up for me.

Best described as an oracle, an *odu* consists of verses of esoteric knowledge along with medicines, rituals and sacrifices which hold the key to all the circumstances and situations, blessings and misfortunes we've been born into. There are a total of 256 *odu* within the sixteen major strands of the Ifa written spiritual teachings – the Yoruba equivalent of the bible.

'I had to dig long and deep for your *odu*, Diane,' Vassa laughed, 'but you'll get so much from it over the years to come.'

She went on to explain that this *odu* provided essential tips about what I needed to be mindful of in my everyday life; my spiritual and emotional life; my health; my destiny; my path of success; my path of relationships; my path of family and my path of victory. But I wasn't feeling particularly victorious. The reading had left me despondent and nervous about whether this Florida business was all a big mistake.

Set in 500 acres of superb West Yorkshire countryside, the park has earned its reputation for being the finest sculpture site in the world, and the UK's leading outdoor art gallery.

My first stop, as usual, was Elizabeth Frink's sinister *Riace Figures*, which remind me of an African masquerade. The four unnervingly lifelike, naked figures, about two metres or so high, hover menacingly amongst the trees, poised for action. White masks have been painted over their dark faces, hiding what they were really up to. Inspired by ancient Greek warrior statues discovered off the coast of Italy, these warriors were, in fact, mercenaries who would fight in return for sacrificial offerings.

Women artists, I believe, produce their best work when freed from the confines of the two-dimensional canvas and the enclosed space of the art gallery. Nikki de Sainte Phalle's *Buddha* − a psychedelic, mosaic and ceramic structure with a third eye that glistens in the Yorkshire sunlight − is a true celebration of colour, fun and spirituality. Barbara Hepworth's *Family of Man*, one of her last works, has a timeless quality to it. The group of nine individual bronze sculptures is all about freedom and harmony. Hepworth said she was passionate that her artistic creations should be *allowed to breathe outdoors*. Adunni, too, loved her work to be displayed in nature, and had spoken to me about how she'd come to hate galleries.

I found myself wondering what the sculptural shrines in Florida's Sacred Orisha Gardens were like, and what sort of energy − if any − they radiated.

After wandering around the park for a couple of hours I began to chill out. After a difficult year with a challenging client-load I was conscious that I was on the verge of burn-out − not good news for a psychotherapist; it's the equivalent, professionally, of a ballet dancer spraining an ankle. One of the Ifa foundation healing rituals that had caught my eye was *Shedding*. This ritual promised to…*remove the negative energy of abuse and spiritual actions…and allow you to retune your vibrational levels to much higher frequencies as well as working with Oshun and Ogun.*

Picking up a certain amount of negative energy from clients was unavoidable; I could do with shedding a ton of it. I wasn't too sure what my vibrational levels were exactly, but I was pretty certain that just about every bit of me could do with retuning – even if, in addition to Oshun, it involved Ogun – the god of metal. And as an early birthday present, I could treat Sally to a ritual or two – something along the lines of attracting a little more romance into her life…

Once home, I read through my Orisha Life Path Divination again. This time it made more sense. A few phrases leapt out at me: *Do not allow anxiety & vulnerability to obscure… Do seek out those with great integrity… Followers of Oshun can show a lack of patience and contentment.*

Well, yes, I had to admit I was impatient. I shouldn't have dismissed the divination so quickly, simply because it wasn't telling me what I'd expected or wanted to hear.

Your 'work' is to keep a peaceful mind and to *try to achieve a higher level of joy.* I certainly couldn't argue with that. My visit to the sculpture park had, indeed, lightened my mood.

Vassa also sent over a prayer to Oshun which sat well with me:

Bring the soft and soothing waters when I am in need
Bring me the ability to successfully manoeuvre the strong currents
of your rivers during the time my life twists and turns.
Move me as necessary while keeping me afloat.
Bring me to the place of more JOY.
Ashe Ashe Ashe

Meet the Ancestors

I HAD TO WAIT for David to set off on his camper van expedition to the Arctic Circle before I could begin my first preparatory ritual. Lasting thirteen minutes precisely, this ritual, designed to help connect me with my ancestors, needed to take place at exactly the same time every day for a week; impossible to achieve amidst my husband's chaotic packing. Not only did David manage to lose his ferry ticket, he almost drove off without his set of golf clubs – a rather necessary accessory, as the purpose of his trip was to play the most northerly golf course in the world.

Once I had the apartment to myself I studied the instructions Vassa had sent over. I lit a white candle, poured some water into a glass, read out the invocation and said aloud, three times, the names of each of my deceased blood relatives on my father's and mother's sides of the family. It felt strange but not unpleasant.

Ancestor worship – or veneration – is big in Africa. Blood relatives, who have gone before, so the general belief goes, still take an active part in the affairs of the world, and have the power to help or hinder the lives of the living and to intercede on their behalf with the gods. The custom also serves to reinforce the values of kinship and filial obedience.

In Buddhism, who or what you're reborn as is pretty much connected to the karma you've generated over previous lifetimes, but karma doesn't come into it where Ifa is concerned. Reincarnation only takes place amongst blood relatives within the same family; when the soul returns it incarnates as a brand new blood relative. The Yoruba give their children names such as Yetunde – meaning *Mother returns*, and Jabatunji – meaning *Father wakes up*.

I've been into a number of homes in Africa densely inhabited by an assortment of relatives – living and deceased. In Benin I almost choked on my pepper soup when my friend casually mentioned that his mother was buried beneath the table we were eating from. When I asked him why he'd interred his mum under their (earthen-floored) kitchen, he said it was where she'd spent most of her time and was her happiest. You can't argue with that.

As I stepped over the threshold of Sally's father-in-law's home in a remote village in Akwa Ibom, the bottle of Gordon's Gin I held out to him as an introductory gift literally exploded in my hand. There was no logical explanation for it. Everyone except me had been delighted by this preternatural libation. It meant, they reassured me, that I met with the approval of the ancestors buried beneath the house. Sally had been to the village several times, but this was my first ever visit and no one had warned me what to expect. After a flight from Lagos followed by a coach journey, we had a long trek through the bush in darkness. An Ekpe masquerade was in progress. Naked men in masks and body paint surreptitiously followed us, concealing themselves behind trees and peering out at us through the vegetation. From time to time they omitted weird, gargling noises and high-pitched catcalls. The masquerade, my brother-in-law warned us, was taboo to females; we were not to look – any woman who caught a glimpse of it would, apparently, be killed. And it was after this, when I *really* needed a drink, that my bottle of Gordon's Gin had spontaneously exploded.

Vassa asked me to send her over my list of deceased blood relatives to enable her to divine the identity of my guardian ancestor while I continued with the daily ritual. When I finally emailed over my meagre list I attempted to explain that whereas Americans tend to be big on ancestors, class-conscious Brits – like my parents – are extremely reluctant to discuss theirs if their ancestors' status and achievements in society have not amounted to much, or there are skeletons in the kinship cupboard; my pitiful handful of dead grandparents, aunties and uncles, were, I told her, the only ancestors I knew anything about.

Actually, I was lying. I couldn't face including my mother's uncle who committed suicide, or my father's deaf and dumb cousin who had been killed when the driver of the breakdown truck towing the faulty motorbike the young man was still seated on braked suddenly. Nor did I wish to include my great grandmother – an obese woman with hair down to her waist and questionable personal hygiene. Something of a battleaxe, she stayed with us just once and expected to be waited on hand and foot. Her husband had been a boxer who had fought in the First World War, and never returned home. Unlike so many of his compatriots, he hadn't lost his life fighting for king and country, he'd run off with a French woman – not that I blame him. The scandal that ensued resulted in the family changing its name. Quite frankly, I felt a bit weird at the idea of worshipping or venerating any of them, let alone having one of them hover over me as a wisdom-dispensing guardian. If anyone in the spirit world was keeping an eye out for me, my gut feeling was that it was my paternal grandmother, Florence, or my son, Sacha.

When Vassa's response arrived it was even briefer than the list I'd sent her:

Let us know which of these ancestors were deceased PRIOR to when you were conceived.

This was starting to get really awkward. Fibbing apart, the only ancestors I knew about PRIOR to my conception were my two young uncles – Peter who died from heart failure at 18, and Georgie, a fighter pilot shot down in the Battle of Britain, aged 21.

Vassa responded with the information that an uncle on my father's side was my guardian ancestor – but it wasn't Peter. She insisted I should go away and do more research – focusing on my paternal grandmother's side of the family.

I plucked up the courage to call my father to make further enquiries. For once, he was surprisingly lucid. I'd been hoping for an intriguing, Lord Lucan-like relative to be lurking in the familial closet, but the reality was infinitely more banal and sad. The number of young men in my family who had died before their time was staggering. I was starting to understand why my parents were less than eager to discuss our forebears. My grandmother, Florence, had three brothers, two of whom had died young. George, a building foreman, died after falling from scaffolding. My father never knew the name of the other uncle who was killed in World War I before he was born. As a child, he remembers there being a photograph of him in soldier's uniform on the mantelpiece.

Eager to confirm my intuition concerning the identity of my guardian ancestor, I lit the white candle, poured water into the glass, and read the invocation which now included these hitherto unknown great uncles. Suddenly the landscape of Northern France flashed through my mind and I recalled driving through that region many years earlier. At a spot where I stopped for lunch I experienced a very strange, déjà-vu-ish sensation. Only later did I learn that I was actually in the Somme region of France where one of the deadliest battles in history had been fought.

I only managed five of the seven days of the ancestor ritual; on the sixth day my car broke down and I couldn't get home in time. I couldn't be bothered to start all over again. My overall hunch was that, if I had one, my guardian ancestor was my great-uncle – the soldier with no name.

Now that I'd established the identity of my guardian *orisha* and was pretty sure about my guardian ancestor, I was equipped and ready to set off for Florida.

Oshun's Welcome

BEYOND THE pond, between the palm trees, the evening sky was ablaze with salmon pinks and vermilion reds. My sister and I were sitting on the mosquito-proofed terrace of our villa, counting the multi-coloured koi carp circling our private water-feature as we tucked into our Duty Frees. Then the vulture appeared.

We'd arrived at the Palm Coast vacation complex, hot and exhausted, the evening before. I had to ask Gee, the friendly manager from Guam, if we could be moved from the villa we'd been assigned. The constant sound of water gushing from the fountain outside would, Sally and I agreed, drive us crazy. Gee obligingly upgraded us to the executive suite without any extra charge; a bedroom each with king-sized beds and bathrooms; a state-of-the-art kitchen; three televisions; no-one overlooking us. We felt like queens.

The vulture perched itself on some rocks a few feet away and stared into the water. Despite the heat, I shivered. Another came, and then another, and another. Resembling hunchbacked, medieval scholars in black gowns and long-beaked, Venetian plague-doctor masks, the four of them strutted around as if they owned the place.

Showing no interest in our ten healthy koi carp, they took leisurely sips of water from the pond, occasionally glancing back in our direction.

I was aware that these ominous-looking creatures have, in recent years, gained a reputation for being one of Africa's unsung heroes. They play a vital role in preventing the spread of disease by clearing away rotting carcasses. Due to indiscriminate poisonings, the use of vulture body parts in traditional medicine, and being deliberately targeted by poachers not wishing to alert authorities to illegally killed big game carcasses, they're teetering on the brink of extinction. Despite knowing this, vultures still unnerve me. And we weren't in Africa; although since arriving in Florida we'd sometimes needed to convince ourselves of that.

During the Paleozoic era Africa and Florida were once part of a supercontinent called Pangaea. When it broke up, over 200 million years ago, North America separated from Africa and a small portion of the African plate stayed stuck to North America and formed the foundation of the Florida Platform. I was amazed at how much the climate and the landscape in Florida looked and felt African; the swathes of dense vegetation; lush mangrove swamps; oleander trees in full bloom; dragon-fruit cacti dwarfed by giant palms. Nile crocodiles have been found in Florida, and earlier that year a breed of South African crocodile was found on a doorstep in Miami. Either these crocodiles were very good swimmers or Africa left Florida with a little more than it bargained for.

The vultures hung around the pond until it grew dark.

'It's a bad omen,' I remarked, as we went back inside.

'I feel OK about them,' Sally responded, unconvincingly.

'Hmm. I certainly don't.'

'I read somewhere they're supposed to be a powerful, protective totem, representing birth, death and new beginnings.'

'Well,' I replied, 'I've seen too many vultures in poor, hot countries hovering over the dead and dying.'

We both fell silent.

Troy, our taxi driver on the two-hour ride from Orlando to Palm Coast had given us the rundown on the perils of Florida, but omitted to mention vultures.

A friendly, stocky guy with light brown hair and a good taste in jazz, Troy filled us in on the rip tides which drag people out to sea; poisonous snakes and spiders; freshwater alligators and sea-water sharks (he boasted that he'd recently surfed through thirty or so of them). Oh, and the newly arrived Zika virus. Temperatures, too, could hit 99°F, Troy said, adding that it was still nothing like the 125°F he'd had to manage while wearing full body armour in Iraq.

'Boy, I had a great time over there,' Troy laughed, when I questioned him about his tour of duty. 'The platoon I was with – we were like a family.'

'Did you get to know many Iraqis?'

'Nah. I didn't do nothing like that. I just stuck with the same bunch of guys for two years. Eating, sleeping, doing everything together. Sometimes I loved 'em, other times I wanted to stab 'em in the face.'

Sally and I exchanged a look.

Troy went on to tell us about his collection of firearms and how he was only permitted to carry a metal cosh in the cab – which he'd had to make use of one night in 'a black, druggy area'.

We didn't dare touch on the subject of Donald Trump.

He was right about the rip tides, though. We'd hired bikes in the morning and cycled to the closest beach, which, according to the resort information, was a five-minute drive, but it took us over an hour. After pedalling past endless launches and speedboats parked in identical canal-side jetties at the ends of manicured gardens owned by members of Florida's abundant community of wealthy retirees, we realised we were lost. With the cheerful willingness to help out that I love about Americans, a friendly couple, also on bikes, insisted on accompanying us a couple of miles to the beach before going on to do their cleaning jobs. Young and well-educated, they said the area was great except there was very little work.

By the time we got to the beach we were desperate for a dip, but the waves were too strong and too high. Even knee-deep in water we could feel ourselves being pulled out to sea. We didn't get as far as checking out the sharks, but we did almost kill ourselves a few times on the way back to the villa, cycling downhill, jetlagged, on bikes with footbrakes rather than handbrakes.

A stone's throw from our villa we spotted a small, inviting slither of sandy beach in a calm part of the river estuary; perfect for swimming. I stopped and asked an elderly couple out walking their dog if there were any alligators in the water. They reassured me they'd lived there all their lives and had never seen one in the river.

'It's safe,' they insisted. 'The river is definitely safe.'

Finally we could have a dip and cool off. I caught up with Sally, who had cycled on ahead, and blurted out the good news.

Grimacing, she pointed to a black and red sign depicting a snake and an alligator along with a warning that it was dangerous to swim in the river.

'Best not risk it,' she said, cycling on.

We stopped to admire a mass of water lilies in a tributary

close to the villa. Lo and behold, grinning up at us was a sizeable alligator. I guess that elderly couple can't have liked Brits very much.

The morning after these birds of prey graced us with their presence we met up with Vassa for the first time. I told her about their visit.

'Great sign, Diane!' she laughed. 'Vultures belong to Oshun. Your guardian *orisha* sent her sacred birds to welcome you and your sister.'

Ola Olu

IF THERE were hills in Florida I'd have described the guy, who clambered out of a battered pick-up truck in a McDonald's car park, as a grizzly old hillbilly. The gentleman in question was Vassa's 'animal man' and she'd pre-arranged this rendezvous to purchase a few of his doves and pigeons for *orisha* rituals.

We were heading for Ola Olu – which means Gift from God – the Sacred Orisha Gardens in Central Florida, forty-five minutes from Vassa's home and an hour's drive from where Sally and I were staying.

In the back seat of Vassa's red Fiat I was trying to avoid getting pecked at by the five doves and two pigeons flapping about in the cage beside me. Sally, meanwhile, was sitting in the front, chatting away to Vassa.

This collection of back-seat endothermic vertebrates had prompted some nervous questioning on my part about animal sacrifice. According to Vassa, it was an occupational necessity – Cubans and Africans, mostly, demanded it. If the sacrifice was a lamb, she assured me, she cooked it and everyone ate it afterwards. From what I could gather, goats, lambs, chickens and birds were the chief fall guys. When I asked her whether my fellow back-seat passengers were destined to meet their maker, too, I didn't receive a direct answer.

'It's crazy,' said Vassa, glancing back at me, 'plants are just as powerful an offering as animals. I don't know why these people won't accept that. Plants have real energy.'

Was she sounding rueful for my vegetarian benefit? Just before picking up the birds, Vassa had pulled into a supermarket and suggested that we might like to purchase some *ebos* (offerings for the *orisha*.) We duly picked up peppers for Ogun; coconuts for Obatala; apples for Shango; melons for Yemonja; egg plants for Oya; oranges and honey for Oshun. I couldn't recall which *orisha* the okra, the plums and the rest of the fruit and vegetables were for – only that Sally and I came out four carrier bags heavier and $57 lighter. I was starting to feel a little anxious about what was in store for us at Ola Olu.

Sally and Vassa continued chatting away to one another about their kids. Vassa was going on about how desperately she was missing her son, who had recently moved to Chicago to take up a fabulously well-paid job. I was desperately missing my son, too. It was his birthday in a few days, and grief was surfacing as it usually does around his anniversaries.

I wasn't the only one feeling left out. The pigeons in the cage were attempting to mate and the flapping of their wings was causing much irritable cooing and pecking on the part of the reluctant-voyeur doves. I fumbled around for my earphones, put my music on random and stared out of the window.

Talking Heads came on. I already had a couple sitting in front of me. A pigeon stuck its tail feathers between the cage bars and crapped on the seat.

And you may ask yourself, well,
How did I get here?

I was one step ahead of these 'Once in a Lifetime' lyrics. I'd
been asking myself that for the past half hour.

Vassa eventually turned off the highway and for ten minutes
we drove down a very bumpy road which cut through dense
countryside.

'I welded them myself,' she proudly informed us, as she
jumped out of the car and unlocked the large bronze gates of
Ola Olu. We drove up a long, grassy track, past an array of carved,
welded and sculpted images of *orisha* scattered amongst the trees
and bushes. Some had vaguely anthropomorphic features; others
were so otherworldly I hadn't a clue quite who or what they
were.

Our first visit to Ola Olu was essentially an introductory one;
an opportunity to take a good look at the Sacred Gardens and to
drop off our *orisha* offerings in readiness for our opening rituals
the following day.

'Feels like we're on another planet,' whispered Sally, as we
transported our offerings from the car and placed them on
trestle tables in a huge, open area situated beneath what was
known as the tree house. The space contained a variety of
ritual requirements – from candles and fetishes to mirrors and
machetes.

Once she'd cleaned the bird crap off the car seat, Vassa
disappeared up a flight of stairs into the tree house. She reappeared
ten minutes later dressed in a long-sleeved white linen shirt and
trousers, leopard-skin-patterned wellington boots, gloves and a
sunhat. It wasn't long before Sally and I, in tee-shirts, shorts and

sandals, realised why Vassa was so covered up; we were getting eaten alive by mosquitoes and a plethora of other bugs, and our 'natural' insect repellent was useless.

'This land belonged to Maroons – escaped African slaves who married native American Indians,' Vassa explained, as she lit some sage sticks in preparation for a shamanic 'smudging' – an age-old traditional practice for 'clearing' the space you're in of any nasties that might be lurking around.

'Before the slaves came it was just the Susquehannock tribe who inhabited the land. Loads of Maroons are buried here; one hell of a turbulent energy matrix. Can you imagine it? When we bought this place we needed to do a great deal of spirit clearing; some of them have stuck around.'

Vassa led us down a long jetty to a sizeable lake. 'We bought this place off Buddhists,' she said, possibly hoping it might help us feel more at home. And it did. The lake was replete with lotus flowers and cranes – both sacred symbols in Buddhism.

'She was of one of *the* Rothschild family. Her husband built the tree house for them as his recovery-from-cancer project… really great people. No pretensions. We've only just paid off the mortgage… Now then; let's take a look the shrines.'

Much like Adunni, Vassa had been inspired to create the Ola Olu shrines under the 'guiding hand' of the *orisha* they represented. She also constructed them with the help of a dedicated group of Ifa priests and priestesses who were under her supervision. For the most part the shrines were abstract. Adunni had once told me that to express these eternal, infinite energies in purely human form would demean the *orisha*.

Vassa led us to a weirdly-shaped vaguely humanoid brown concrete structure with five long limbs stretching up towards the heavens.

'Here's my *IyaMoopo*. The goddess of Indigo sculpture I built in Suzanne Wenger's honour.'

'Wow!' Sally gazed up at it. 'Very striking.'

'Her belly's thirteen foot in diameter.' Vassa brushed away bits of moss that clung to its sides. 'You have to let the sculpture allow you to create it.'

I didn't dare say that it wasn't a patch on Adunni's own *IyaMoopo* – but it was a gesture that I was certain would have pleased the High Priestess.

Sally commented on the different species of butterfly in the gardens, prompting Vassa to list the variety of wildlife that had been sighted there over the years, which included snakes, owls, alligators, egrets, racoons, brown bears and even a black panther. I looked nervously around.

Vassa must have noticed that the heat and the overall weirdness of the place were starting to affect us novices.

'Time for some late lunch,' she called out as she disappeared into the tree house to prepare some food, leaving Sally and me to wander around the gardens.

'Well, does it remind you of the Sacred Groves in Oshogbo?' Sally asked, when we were out of earshot.

'A bit, but the atmosphere here is more heightened, less peaceful.'

'Perhaps the energy is more intense because the shrines are condensed into a much smaller area.'

'Maybe. I guess that would make the *orisha* emanations more potent.' We sat on a bench and soaked them up.

Back in England, when I was planning this visit, on a Skype call with Vassa she'd suggested that we might like to stay in the Ola Olu tree house. Envisaging this to be an accessed-by-ladder, mosquito-infested, wooden shed stuck in a tree with a Calor gas ring and sleeping bags on the floor, I declined. But when we walked inside this graceful wooden edifice on stilts I felt a twinge of regret that I didn't take her up on her generous offer. With windows on all sides, an open-plan kitchen, massive living room, bedroom, bathroom plus shower, this tastefully furnished residence had aircon and every mod con you could possibly need. All that was 'tree-housey' about it was the fact it was made of wood and surrounded by trees.

Sally and I sat at a long, wooden table consuming masses of water, and stared in wonder at the African images, effigies and artefacts which adorned the surfaces and walls. Vassa chatted away while preparing the food. I decided I liked her. She was open and warm, with a great sense of humour. It felt safe to confess that I'd failed to complete the ancestor-connecting ritual she'd advised me to do before coming over. Vassa looked up from her food, and proposed something completely unexpected.

'Before we leave today we're going to perform a ritual to put a stop to this pattern of young men in your family dying before their time.'

After lunch Vassa led me to a glade of trees which had gourds of assorted colours, shapes and sizes hanging from their branches.

'This is where the *iyamis* hang out.'

'*Iyamis*? What are they?'

'Primordial Mothers; a collection of powerful female energies that have been with us since the beginning of time. *Iyamis* control birth and rebirth. They make it their business to see to the protection of the family.'

She pointed to a shrine close by. Half above and half below the ground, it half resembled a woman.

'That's a shrine to the *orisha*, Onile – the Ifa equivalent of Mother Earth.'

Vassa recited an *orike* – a prayer of praise in Yoruba – and instructed me to say a prayer out loud asking the *iyamis* to protect present and future generations of young men in our family. I had a weep for my Sacha, then, mindful that I had five nephews I was extremely fond of, did as I was told – albeit self-consciously.

A breeze started up; gourds hanging from the branches clattered together.

'That's a great sign,' Vassa said, patting my head.

Sally looked relieved. She was thinking about her son. In the treetops above us, birds began squawking and flapping about.

Vassa smiled. 'It's OK. The Mothers have heard your prayer.'

Spaced Out

WE MADE our way back to Ola Olu the following morning. Parked beyond the gates, awaiting our arrival, was a white limousine, which snaked slowly behind us up the driveway. Once we'd parked up Vassa introduced us to our fellow visitors.

'Sally and Diane meet Norton and his mom.'

Meeting a trainee astronaut who had just driven down from Utah and was on his way to NASA, via Miami, was intriguing; the fact he was an extremely handsome, charming, energetic Afro-American with a perfect six-pack was thrilling; but learning that he'd come all the way to Ola Olu to dig up a goat's head was, quite frankly, jaw-dropping.

Norton's gum-chewing mom settled down on a sofa beneath the tree house and asked Sally if she knew Haringey, in North London; she had a friend who lived there. Mom had difficulty walking and had only come to Ola Olu at Norton's insistence.

Norton, meanwhile, was hunting around for a spade.

'Why do you need to dig the head up?' I asked. He looked

at me, shyly.

'Well... I...er...I wanna place it on my altar. The goat was slaughtered when I got initiated three months ago. You have to leave the head in the earth for a few months to decompose.'

'Oh, right. So who is your guardian *orisha*, then?'

'Oko.'

According to the Ifa creation myth, Oko dragged his huge testicles along the ground and vegetation grew. I chose not to mention this.

'He's the *orisha* of the soil, isn't he?'

'Yeah, that's him,' Norton replied. 'Oko wants his sacrifices placed in the ground. He's also one of the two legs of the wisdom god, Obatala. That makes him all about balance and stability.'

'I can see why an astronaut would need to feel grounded!'

Healing and maintaining the spiritual wellbeing of the home and family were also part of Oko's job spec. I'd noticed the worried glances Norton had been giving grumpy Mom, who clearly had issues, not only around mobility but about being here at all.

Vassa wandered over to the trestle tables and picked up a bottle of Malibu and a packet of cigars.

'OK, let's go. We're gonna pay Eshu a visit and open up.'

Eshu's role is quite seminal in Ifa. He's the messenger who delivers prayers and offerings to Olodumare (the Ifa version of God – with a capital G) and who oversees the workings of both humans and *orisha*. He's also responsible for opening every ceremony and ritual. Before any communication is made with an *orisha* a tribute must first be paid to him. Something of a trickster, he was believed by Christian missionaries to be the devil – and, with his appetite for booze and cigars, no doubt they still believe this.

Vassa led us through undergrowth to a dark brown mound

with ugly facial features superimposed onto it – like a massive version of Mr Potato Head from *Toy Story 3*.

Norton was hovering patiently around the shrine, clutching a bottle of Smirnoff, waiting for us to join him. He was keen to get the ritual over with so he could get digging. Mom was sitting on a nearby chair looking bored.

Vassa instructed us to offer libations to Eshu. This involved either spitting a little of the alcohol onto the shrine and swallowing the rest, or pouring it on directly. Vassa handed us the bottle of Malibu. Sally and I opted for the spitting and swallowing, while Norton, showing more restraint, poured his vodka straight on. My sister and I liked the taste of the Malibu and tried to get away with as many libations as was decently possible. Vassa lit up a cigar and offered one to us. Sally and I looked at each other. She'd given up smoking but chewed nicotine gum when stressed. I *loved* cigars but I hadn't smoked for years. The devil won.

'I really fancy a puff,' grinned Sally.

'Sod it, so do I. Let's share one.' We took it in turns to inhale deeply and could have continued in this vein for some time, but our more abstemious buddies were keen to move on. Vassa placed her half-smoked cigar in Eshu's 'mouth.'

Norton began his digging while we moved from shrine to shrine, depositing the appropriate piece of fruit or veg in accordance with each *orisha*'s preferred (vegetarian) offering. We couldn't understand a word of the *orike* Vassa recited at each shrine, but joined in with her *Ashe* at the end – a grateful acknowledgement of the power and blessing of the *orisha*; a kind of Ifa 'Amen'.

In the course of dishing out our *orisha* offerings, the only shrine that resonated for me, was, predictably, Oshun's – which backed onto the lake. Represented as a life-sized, coppery-looking, vaguely female form, the goddess had heart shapes where her breasts would be, and peacock feathers sprouting from the top of her head. I was happy to deposit oranges and honey at her 'feet'.

Vassa was busy dishing out tuna salad for herself and Sally, and I was peeling a boiled egg, when Norton, looking hot and frustrated, poked his head around the door. He couldn't find his goat's head.

'I've been digging just where I buried it,' he fretted, waving a compass at us. I've dug down three feet. It isn't there but I can smell it!'

The visual of a decomposing goat's head – not to mention the olfactory element – put me right off my egg salad.

'Ask Orumila!' instructed Vassa. Norton ran off downstairs to the divination plate to consult Orumila, the *orisha* of knowledge. But fifteen minutes later he was back again, shaking his head.

'What do you expect me to do about it?' asked Vassa, with a hint of irritation in her voice.

'You tell me,' he grinned. 'You're the expert.'

'Maybe it's too soon. Try Ogun!'

He nodded and disappeared. I was starting to feel sorry for Norton. Had he driven all this way with his miserable mom for nothing?

When we came down from the tree house after lunch he was staring ruefully at the divination plate.

'Ogun says to come back in six months.'

'OK,' Vassa nodded sagely. 'That makes sense. You're still not ready.'

We watched and waved as a relieved-looking Mom and a

dejected-looking Norton climbed into the white limousine and set off for the Kennedy Space Centre, empty-handed.

Vassa dropped us off outside our villa later that afternoon. Sally and I changed straight into our swimsuits and dived into the pool. The day had left us feeling out of our depth and lost for words. But more weirdness was to follow.

My sister was hanging out her costume after the swim, and I was in the shower, when I heard the glass doors between the living room and the terrace slam shut. Sally suddenly screamed.

'There's a black mamba on the terrace!'

'It must have come a really long way,' I yelled back. 'Black mambas are from sub-Saharan Africa.'

'I'm going to Reception for help,' she shouted, rushing out the door.

The snake was about five feet long, and, from where I was standing in my hastily-wrapped towel, without any discernible markings. I was thankful we'd closed the glass doors before we went out to swim. It could have slithered in and hid – well – heaven only knows where; between the bed sheets?

Sally returned, looking perturbed. Reception had told her not to worry, insisting it could only be a garter snake, and that they'd send Maintenance over immediately.

'It's nothing like a garter snake,' I told her. 'Sacha used to have one. They're much smaller and have markings.'

Maintenance arrived a few minutes later in a golf buggy. He was wearing a blue uniform and holding a rubbish pick-up pole and a large white plastic bin.

After taking one look at our snake he said he'd have to fetch a bigger implement as it could be venomous.

Maintenance returned five minutes later with a garden rake in tow. The snake clearly wasn't going to give in easily and Maintenance had to fence with it for some time. The large, silver crucifix hanging around his neck swung from side to side. When, finally, he managed to get the snake into the bin and was about to tighten the lid, it reared up – *Jaws*-like – knocking the lid back off and wriggling away again. Even I was screaming now. Finally, finally, he managed to get it back into the bin and secure the lid.

While Maintenance cleared up on the terrace I Googled *snakes of Florida*.

'There are fifty species of snake in Florida, only five are venomous and none of the venomous ones are black,' I told him.

He glanced at me incuriously. 'Is that so?'

I found it surprising he didn't know this already; being able to identify the venomous snakes in your home state was a no-brainer, I would have thought.

'We've had an alligator in one of the ponds here,' Maintenance said, 'but I've never seen a snake on a terrace before.'

What we couldn't understand – and neither could he – was how it had got through the taut, mosquito-protective mesh and onto the terrace in the first place.

'What are you going to do with it?' I asked.

'God willing, I'm gonna drive him to the woods and release him. Non-venomous snakes are a godsend to us. They protect us from the venomous ones.'

'How?'

'They eat them.'

'Oh, right.'

Snakes, we later learnt, were sacred to Oshun, too. We wondered if this visitation had anything to do with our offerings to the goddess earlier that day.

At Home with the Neimarks

PHIL, VASSA'S partner, wanted to meet us; we wanted to meet Phil. So one evening we were invited to their home for dinner. Sally and I cycled out to a garish, modern development called The European Village to purchase a gift to take with us.

On our way there we were unpleasantly surprised by the sheer number of *Vote Trump Make America Great Again!* placards sprouting up from the lawns of palatial homes. Most news reports in the UK had led us to believe that the majority of Trump supporters lived in trailer parks. There wasn't a *Vote Clinton* sign anywhere to be seen.

The European Village was an enclave of faux-European, yellow, pink and terracotta buildings containing shops, restaurants and apartments, which encircled a piazza strewn with naff-looking plaster casts of ancient Greek statues. Once we'd purchased our dinner-guest gifts we parked ourselves outside a very un-European Mexican bar, ordered cold beers and tacos and tried to reassure ourselves that the American public couldn't possibly allow a faux-politician like Trump anywhere near the White House.

Phil was sitting in the front passenger seat when Vassa pulled up outside the villa to collect us. A warm, friendly, frail-looking man, seventeen years older than his wife, Phil had twinkly, wizard-like eyes and an infectious, magician's laugh. A couple of years ago he suffered a stroke and was now pretty much housebound. Much of his divining work had to be done online.

En route to the house, Vassa made a detour via some Floridian swamps to give us a glimpse of their local bird life. She slowed down as we passed a large, newish house that Phil claimed was where the Bonnie and Clyde shoot-out had taken place. He asked us if we'd heard of them. Who hadn't? But I was perplexed, not only because the house looked quite modern, but also because I thought the final shoot-out had happened in Louisiana. It transpired, however, that a young Missouri couple, who were 'armed and dangerous' had earned the nickname Bonnie and Clyde when they went on a multistate crime spree earlier in the year which included kidnappings and robberies in Alabama, Georgia and Florida. Although they themselves hadn't killed anyone, 'Clyde' was shot and killed by gun-happy County Sheriff deputies, and 'Bonnie' wounded.

We pulled up outside an impressively large, detached house in a wooded close. In the porch we were greeted by three noisy dogs of assorted breeds, ages and sizes. Once inside, my sister and I were taken aback by the sheer enormity and stylishness of the place. Massive oil paintings depicting an assortment of *orisha* hung on the walls – commissioned, we were told, from an artist living in England. African carvings, bronzes and sculptures adorned the gymnasium-sized living room. Wall-to-wall sliding glass doors led out onto an enormous glass-ceilinged conservatory crammed full of luscious, tropical plants. In the centre of the conservatory the decent-sized swimming pool was open to the stars.

'This is the most beautiful house I've ever seen,' whispered Sally. At which point the skies opened and we watched as huge drops of rain created tiny fountains on the surface of the indigo-coloured pool.

We presented Phil and Vassa with the tropical plant and decent bottle of New Zealand wine that we'd chosen for them in the European Village, but dotted around the house were several much larger, more colourful versions of our little plant, and it transpired that neither of them drank alcohol.

The Russian housekeeper was away so Vassa prepared our meal in the open-plan, designer kitchen. We, meanwhile, sat on comfortable, king-sized sofas and chatted to Phil as he fed treats to his overweight little dog. Our somewhat stilted, platitudinous conversation livened up when I returned from a trip to the loo, wet all over, having mistaken the bidet 'up' jet button for the flush. Sally got the giggles; my cue to switch the conversation to a more serious note. I asked Phil how he came to be involved in Ifa.

It all began, he told us, in 1974. He was thirty-three years old, married (to his previous partner), living in Chicago and working in finance. Although rich and successful, his life was governed by fear; he angsted over just about everything. This all changed, however, when, on a visit to Miami, he and his wife tagged along with some friends who were going to see a *babalawo* (priest) for a Life Path reading. Just for the fun of it, Phil agreed to have a reading, too.

The *odu* that came up during his divination told the story

of a young African *oba*, (king) who, through another's act of treachery, lost his title, his wealth and his wife and was forced into exile in the wilderness. Battling hunger and the elements, he grew weaker and weaker. Eventually, after giving up all hope of ever being restored to power, he stripped naked, lit a fire and burnt his royal robes to keep himself warm.

Meanwhile, in a neighbouring kingdom, an old *oba* had recently passed away. The *babalawos* consulted Orunmila, the *orisha* of knowledge, who predicted that the new *oba* would be found naked and alone beside a plume of smoke. When the *babalawos* saw the smoke rising from the deposed young king's fire, they rushed into the wilderness to welcome him. He was proclaimed their new *oba* and his wealth and glory were restored.

The *babalawo* in Miami told Phil that he, too, would soon lose everything. But the loss would enable him to find his correct path in life. And if he sacrificed to Orunmila, (who was the main player in this oracle) he would become even greater, wealthier and happier than before.

Spooked and sceptical at the same time, Phil decided he'd try to get his head around this whole business of Ifa so that he could prove it was phoney. He contacted Dr William Bascom, a professor of anthropology at the University of Berkeley. To his amazement, this eminent professor – the western world's foremost authority on Ifa – appeared to take it all very seriously. Eventually, Dr Bascom said to him, 'Mr Neimark, all I can tell you is that it works.'

As the *babalawo* predicted, in the year that followed Phil's reading he lost all his wealth and his marriage fell apart. And, like the young *oba* in the oracle, he found himself alone in the wilderness.

I looked around at the luxurious home and costly artefacts on display. Vassa mentioned earlier that their more valuable items were stowed away in the safe. What with all of this, the tree house and the land at Ola Olu, these days, the Neimarks were doing very nicely, thank you.

As if he'd read my thoughts, Phil added with a grin, 'that old *babalawo* was right. I got it all back again, and more.' But not before he'd started to take the practice and study of Ifa seriously.

The upswing in his fortunes, he noticed, came about when his outlook on life became more holistic and he began to embrace the spiritual alongside the material. He also met Vassa. Phil schooled her not only in business – she was setting up as an interior architect at the time – but also in Ifa. She took to it immediately, and before long found herself inexplicably drawn to working in metal. Vassa's artistic talent, in my opinion, lies in her metalwork. It was hardly surprising that her guardian *orisha* turned out to be Ogun, that tough old god of iron.

Eventually, a fifth-generation African *babalawo* initiated Phil as an *oluwo* – the highest level a *babalawo* can hope to attain. Phil claimed that these days he no longer feels afraid of anything.

We were called to the table. Vassa had prepared a pumpkin and sweet potato dish for me, as they were having fish. She turned to Phil.

'These ladies have met Suzanne Wenger, you know.'

'What a woman!' enthused Phil, as he poured us a glass of our New Zealand wine. 'You're very fortunate.' We chatted for a while about Adunni – whom neither of them had met – and how fewer and fewer American devotees were attending the Oshun Festival for reasons of personal safety.

I was keen to know what had led them to create the Sacred Orisha Gardens. Phil explained that once they'd both fully committed to the path of Ifa, they began to realise that the vibe of the Cuban-orientated Santería/Lucumí practised in downtown Chicago didn't feel right. The patriarchal structure was too controlling and they were unhappy that the rituals mainly took place in insalubrious basements and garages. They decided to branch out on their own and set up their first Sacred Orisha Garden in fifteen acres of land between two national forest preserves in Bloomington, Indiana – a four-hour drive south from Chicago.

'It was in Bloomington that I really began channelling Suzanne's vision of creating shrines and gardens for each of the *orisha*,' explained Vassa, refilling our glasses. 'I got into welding, and built myself a workshop. I also began to communicate telepathically with Suzanne. I felt she was sending me energy waves of ideas.'

'Like Suzanne, we were creating a fresh new path for Ifa,' added Phil.

But they found the winters harsh, and after fourteen years of battling with snow and ice, decided they wanted to be in a location where they could work all year round. Guided, once again, by Orunmila, around the time of 9/11 they moved their entire outfit, shrines included, to a piece of land on the edges of the Ocala National forest in Central Florida, which is now Ola Olu.

In the hallway were pictures of their son and daughter – both radiant-looking creatures in their twenties. I was curious to know where they fitted in. Phil told us that the kids, too, were brought up in the ways of Ifa, and still practised it – but not with the same intensity as their parents. It didn't surprise me to learn that they were home-schooled – God only knows what Evangelical or Creationist teachers might have made of their beliefs. But the home-schooling, we were told, wasn't to avoid any religious bullying. Their son, Phil explained, was a very talented tennis player and needed a flexible timetable which would accommodate training. Phil devoted a great deal of time, money and energy into getting his son properly coached, and in taking him to tournaments all over the US. To his disappointment, the young man decided against making a professional career out of it.

Somehow, I found it hard to reconcile tennis tournaments with Ifa worship.

I asked Vassa, as I helped her to clear the table, if it had been hard work raising a family at the same time as establishing the foundation and constructing the gardens at Ola Olu.

'We managed OK but it can't have been easy for the kids,' she replied, with a grin, 'growing up with a mom who keeps goats testicles in the fridge.'

Maze Meditation

'DOING THE work,' Vassa insisted, 'brings you to the place.'

I wasn't quite sure what 'the place' was that 'the work' would take us to but I was hoping that walking the Ola Olu labyrinth might get us there.

We were already feeling hot and wiped out after 'doing the work' all morning. 'The work' was 'shedding' and involved 'peeling off the layers'. We'd been peeling off the layers all right. We were each presented with a large white onion, and with each layer that we peeled we were encouraged to shed 'whatever was stuck' in our lives, and to 'delete old programmes.'

Before the onion peeling we were given eggs to hold in each hand and told to channel all our negative life experiences into them. We were then instructed to stand on the end of the jetty with our backs to the lake and chuck the eggs over our shoulders into the water. This fun ritual was all about 'releasing' our baggage, and we both felt a little lighter for it. After that we sat around a bowl of burning ghee, sage and cow dung (don't

146

ask) and stared into the flames as we continued to 'let go'.

The previous night, Vassa had handed us lumps of *Ifa Ose* – otherwise known as African black soap – to 'cleanse' ourselves in preparation for the shedding rituals. The soap was made from shea butter and dried plants with 'a high vibrational level' for cleansing the *ori* – our physical and spiritual head – and 'pockets of the body where darkness can reside.' Actually, it was dark brown rather than black, and unfortunately resembled fecal matter; definitely something you wouldn't leave in your soap dish if you had visitors, or risk taking through customs. Thankfully, it had no odour, was soft on the skin and pleasant to use – providing you kept your eyes closed.

The time had come for my sister and me to walk the labyrinth. We looked around for Vassa; we needed our instructions. She was standing beside the trestle tables under the tree house chatting to her sister Carol, who had come to buy sage sticks.

'You're gonna love the maze,' Carol smiled, reassuringly. I attempted a convincing nod. We were sweating in our bug-proof wellies, and the water in our bottles was getting hot.

A pleasant, pretty woman who used to work in the glamour industry, Carol now helped terminally ill people achieve 'a good death.' She told us that the day before she'd taken a retired professor dying with cancer around all his favourite university haunts for the last time. Vassa decided to give Carol the sage sticks for her birthday.

'Trump's a fucker!' Carol exclaimed. We replied that we couldn't stomach him either. Their other sister, whom we hadn't met, was a born-again Trump-supporting, gun-toting Christian. Needless to say, the three sisters didn't always see eye-to-eye.

Carol was on her fourth marriage, and Lee, her latest husband, who was a pilot, had tagged along, too. An affable guy with a baseball cap and a Freddie Mercury moustache, Lee had a rather bemused expression on his face. I wanted to ask him what he made of Ola Olu, but I didn't get the chance.

Vassa told us to choose a walking stick from a motley collection of hand-carved African ones, then handed us each a smoking sage stick. I inwardly groaned. My eyes were already sore from peeling the onion, and from sage, ghee and dung smoke.

'Every step you take, let go of a layer from the past and 'go deeper,' she called out after us, as she sent us on our way.

The labyrinth, which Vassa had constructed herself, consisted of 256 steps and 333 shrubs that ran alongside them and led to 'the vortex' – in other words, its centre.

When you walk the labyrinth at Ola Olu with intention, the Ifa Foundation website claimed, you will be letting go of your inner obstacles – stress, sadness, negative thoughts, negative feelings, fears. As we set off, the whole lot of them were still clinging on to me – along with mosquitoes and sweat. Each one of the 256 steps I was treading had been engraved with its own unique *odu* symbol. These ancient patterns in binary code represented an aspect of 'the Calabash of Existence' – or the universe according to Ifa. A *babalawo* or an *iyanifa* – a priest or a priestess – made it their life's work to learn the meaning of each of the 256 *odu*, and to acquire the ability to interpret them with relevance. But to the uninitiated like me these domino-like symbols were incomprehensible. I decided, instead, to focus on the 'personal labyrinth meditation'.

Every now and then Vassa broke off chatting to Carol and Lee and rushed over with her camera to take pictures of us – which didn't exactly aid my concentration. Then, without realising, Sally, who was way ahead of me, accidentally set fire to one of the shrubs with the tip of her sage stick. The vegetation was dry and there was a slight breeze. The consequences didn't bear thinking about. Not wishing to be remembered as the sisters who reduced Ola Olu to ashes and brought the wrath of the *orisha* down on their heads I had no choice but to douse the burning bush with the remains of my precious water and pray that Vassa was looking the other way.

On the drive there that morning, Vassa had been telling us about her Irish and Greek ancestry. Her guardian ancestor, apparently, was a Greek labyrinth builder and walker from many centuries ago. 'He gave me the labyrinth vision and has helped me to see it through to construction,' she explained. The shrines at Ola Olu were clearly Vassa's personal interpretation of Ifa, inspired by her guardian ancestor and created with the aid of Ogun, her guardian *orisha*, who, from what she'd told us, worked through her like a rumbustious muse.

I was supposed to be gazing into the mirror of my soul, but as I continued my journey through the maze I started to feel more like the poor old minotaur, plodding impatiently around his Knossos labyrinth looking for a way out. Instead of directing itself inwards, my labyrinth meditation drifted into the virtually impenetrable maze that was Ifa itself. I had no problem, I realised, with the Sixteen Truths of Ifa – in fact, apart from the God bit, I found them impressively Buddhist:

1. This is a benevolent universe created by a benevolent god
2. You need have no fear
3. There is a single creative force (God)
4. There is no devil
5. It is your birthright to be joyful, successful and loved
6. Personal empowerment is your engine for success and fulfilment
7. You are part of the universe in a literal, not figurative way

8. Character determines outcome
9. All supremacy is evil
10. You must never initiate harm to another human being
11. You must never harm the universe of which you are a part
12. Discrimination is personally and culturally destructive
13. Diversity is the hallmark of Olodumare's (God's) creation
14. You select your destiny
15. Divination provides the road map to your destiny
16. Balance, growth and wisdom provide your empowerment

What I struggled with was trying to reconcile all of Ifa's different branches, manifestations and add-ons. While its divination rituals largely remained intact following the Middle Passage, the diaspora had led to such a variety of local interpretations – in the New World, especially.

Since the mid 20th century, Ifa-related practices had undergone a phenomenal surge in popularity in the ethnic melting pot of the United States. Santería, the Catholic/Ifa mix, first appeared in the US when Puerto Ricans began flooding in during the Forties and Fifties, followed, soon after, by Cuban refugees in the Sixties, who brought with them Lucumí, their version of Santería.

Black Power activists in the Seventies claimed it was a black religion exclusively for black people – despite Ifa purists insisting that all people on the earth, of every colour, were born in Ilé-Ifè and Obatala, one of the primary *orisha*, was often depicted as being white.

Many Afro-American followers of Kemeticism (the modern worship of ancient Egyptian gods) insisted that the age-old

Egyptian belief system had its origins in Ifa worship, which had been brought to Egypt by migrating Yoruba many thousands of years earlier. More recently, the Afro-Brazilian, saint-heavy Candomblé had made its presence felt, and Haitian refugees had introduced Voodoo – a mixture of Yoruba and Congo gods, Freemasonry and Catholicism, with a bit of magic thrown in.

Practitioners like Vassa and Phil believed they were taking Ifa back to its traditional, liberal African roots. With the establishment of their foundation, they'd reintroduced the Yoruba concept of *ori*: the belief that our head possesses a divine as well as a physical aspect – long ignored by Catholicised diasporic practitioners. They also re-established the Ifa tradition of complete gender equality, and theirs was the first organisation in North America to initiate a fully fledged female *iyanifa* and an openly gay *babalawo*.

But these achievements, too, came at a price. As I dragged myself around the maze, I mulled over the challenges they'd faced in their efforts to establish their version of Ifa in North America. Given a leaning in many parts of the States towards Christian Fundamentalism, their brand of 'pagan' worship was hardly welcomed with open arms, and it had taken them a number of years to be officially registered as a bona fide religion. Vassa had spoken to me about death threats the pair had received from rival practitioners, jealous of Ola Olu's success. She attributed Phil's recent bout of serious health issues to his being the target of destructive *ju-ju* practices.

When I finally reached the vortex of the labyrinth I was a tad disappointed to discover there was nothing particularly unusual about it – just a few taller shrubs. No chance here of being whisked off to another dimension of reality.

Sally had already arrived and was busy glugging back water.

'I've run out of stuff to shed,' she whispered, conspiratorially.

'I'm knackered and I'm starving.'

'Me too,' I replied, grabbing her bottle of water and explaining why my own was empty.

Daedalus had constructed his labyrinth at Knossos so cleverly that even he struggled to find a way out. And when he eventually succeeded, King Minos kept him locked up in a tower to safeguard the labyrinth's secret. The great inventor eventually managed to escape, but he paid a high price: the wax on his son Icarus' 'escape wings' melted when he disobeyed his father by flying too close to the sun. As the exit to the maze finally came into view I caught myself wondering whether Adunni ever yearned to find a way out of the Sacred Groves, or Vassa these Sacred Orisha Gardens. When your religion has become not only the medium through which you, as an artist, express yourself, but also your livelihood, and you have accumulated followers and acquired dependents, it isn't that easy to walk away from it all – however much you may, at times, yearn to.

Birdlife

I LOATHE seeing birds in cages. Since our first outing to Ola Olu the fate of the backseat birds had been on my mind. The pigeons were still in the cage, but on our subsequent visits there I'd clocked the ominous absence of the doves. I hoped they'd been set free at an Ifa wedding ceremony and not had their necks wrung as an *orisha* sacrifice; I didn't want to ask. It was a relief when Vassa announced one day that we were going to perform a ritual which involved releasing the poor old pigeons.

We gathered around the cage on the trestle table. Vassa explained that, first off, we needed to cradle the pigeons while channelling all our sorrows and sufferings into them; she would then take them from us, one at a time, and recite an orike as she stroked us with the pigeon's wings before handing them back to us to release. And as the pigeon was released, all our anguish, she assured us, would be released, too.

I couldn't help feeling slightly miffed that for this apparently important Ifa ritual, Sally and I had been designated common or garden pigeons – labelled sky rats by some. I wasn't expecting an eagle or a peacock, but a dove would have been nice.

Vassa opened the cage and handed the larger, male pigeon to Sally and the smaller, female, to me. I admit I was nervous. I've had a few dodgy encounters with birds. As a kid, I was savagely pecked on the lip by our budgie, and a couple of years ago a mallard duck in Braemar bit my hand while attempting to steal my sandwich. More recently, a male swan guarding a nest on the Bridgewater Canal had mistaken my white coat for another swan and started attacking me. But I knew I was being pathetic. This poor little pigeon was even more nervous than I was.

Sally's pigeon settled into her cupped hands and remained immobile as she stroked it. My pigeon wriggled around like crazy. I could feel her tiny heart pounding away in her chest. She was frightened. I felt dreadful, suddenly. What right had I to pour all my shit into this poor creature? I started to shake. She flapped her wings and tried to take off. Was this working the wrong way around? Perhaps the pigeon was channelling her fear into me? Suddenly I was overcome with such intense distress that I let out an involuntary scream and released her. She fell to the ground, immobile. I was so upset I ran off in tears and sat on a bench bawling my eyes out.

In the distance, I could see Vassa taking Sally's pigeon from her and wiping her all over with his wings. As if in a trance, Sally took the bird back again and as she released him she tottered around and almost fell over. Her pigeon, too, flew about a metre in the air and then fell, leaden, to the ground.

'Are they dead?' I asked Sally when she eventually wandered over to the bench, still looking dazed.

'I don't know. I'll go and look in a moment. Are you all right?'

'No, I'm not'.

'That was so weird,' she said. 'When Vassa stroked me with the wings it was like I was having an electric shock. I was gulping for air and reeling when I released him… It felt really primal.'

Before I could stop her, Vassa had crept up on me with her camera. At that moment, having my picture taken was the very last thing I needed.

'Are those pigeons dead?' I demanded, with an accusatory note in my voice.

'They took some heavy stuff from you both,' Vassa said, not answering the question. 'One time I did this ritual for a woman with some real crazy hangups. When she released her pigeon this owl came out of nowhere, swooped down, snatched it up in its beak and flew off with it.'

I dried my eyes, blew my nose and plucked up the courage to investigate the fate of the pigeons. To my amazement, they were still alive, lumbering around the undergrowth, looking drunk, befuddled and unlikely to become airborne any time soon; perfect predator fodder. Vassa handed us a bag of grain and we fed them.

The following day I headed straight for that same patch of undergrowth. There was no sign of either the pigeons or their feathers. What a relief. An atmosphere of calm prevailed until the evening, when Vassa emailed the photograph she'd taken of me on the bench the day before, along with a caption: *Can you see your ancestor witch?*

'What do you think Vassa means by your ancestor witch?' Sally asked, studying the photograph carefully. We were both feeling a bit spooked. Although we sometimes joked about our wacky rituals we knew there was no denying Ifa was powerful.

'I'm really not sure. I thought she was referring to a crow or some creature in the trees behind me, but I can't see anything in that photograph.'

Sally looked perturbed. 'I made an etching, years ago, it was at art school, I think, of a woman and a bird. That picture flashed through my mind as I released my pigeon yesterday. The scenario was virtually identical. It's hard to put into words what I felt…it was such a strange sensation…'

'Suzanne…Adunni experienced something similar. She even had a name for it: *forward memory*.' I went on to share a confusing exchange that had taken place, years ago, between myself and Adunni – well, it was confusing for me, at least.

Adunni was watching a pair of waxbills pecking away at scraps of cassava in the dusty Oshogbo street outside her house.

'We live beyond time,' she pronounced, suddenly.

'I'm not sure I understand.'

'This house, for example,' she said, gesticulating behind her, with a hint of impatience. 'I *knew* it before I set eyes upon it. Years ago, in Vienna, I'd dreamt about baroque, Brazilian-style buildings – just like this one, built by freed slaves returning to their homeland. I'd even made expressionist sketches of them. Forward memory I call it.'

'Is this 'forward memory' a kind of clairvoyance?'

'Clairvoyance is simply seeing into the future. Forward memory is remembering it.'

I was struggling to understand. 'Some mystics believe that at a deep level we all possess a consciousness that exists beyond space and time…'

'They do indeed.'

'…And there's a concept in Buddhism known as *Kuon ganjo* – the idea that there is an eternal, infinite place which exists outside any temporal framework. Is it something like that?'

'To a certain extent, but forward memory is more visceral. When I first stumbled upon the ancient priests and priestesses in Ede, who were to become my ritual mothers and fathers, my love for them already existed. I *felt* it – even though I'd never met them before. They *knew* me already, too, and they *remembered in advance* that I would dedicate the remainder of my life to preserving and creating shrines to the *orisha*.'

'You believe time is non-linear, then?'

'I most certainly do. This level of consciousness, in which time and space are relative, is known to the Yoruba as *lae lae*.'

'*Lae lae… Lae lae…*' Deep in thought, Sally repeated it over and over as if committing the concept to memory.

'But not everything was a forward memory for her,' I continued. 'Only snapshots. On another occasion she said it had never crossed her mind that she would end up in Nigeria; it came about by itself, like a picture painting itself.'

Sally laughed. 'Funny. That's just how it was with me.'

Sisterhood

'TRIPS TO Europe were frequent in those days', Vassa sighed, with a note of regret in her voice. 'When we went to London we'd stay in the Ritz...But Phil doesn't like to travel so much now...'

We were in her office admiring a photograph of their younger, trendier-looking 1980s-selves draped around one another in a pigeon-strewn square in Rome – the city where they married.

'Come, take a look at this.' She led us down some steps into a large, windowless basement area. 'This here is my workshop. I'm so proud of it.'

And she had every reason to be, I thought, as we stepped inside an Ifa worshipper's goldmine. The shelves were stacked with *orisha* effigies, horsehair wands, divining trinkets, bottles of herbs, pots and potions and all nature of African artefacts, which she sold online to practitioners around the globe. Half a dozen or so doves flapped about in a cage bigger than the one at Ola Olu. There was something distinctly medieval about this cellar space; it was how I imagined an alchemist's study would have looked. The longer I spent with Vassa the more she intrigued me.

I had hundreds of questions on the tip of my tongue, but I asked only one: what or who was this so-called ancestor witch of mine? We filed back into the office. Vassa scrolled through hundreds of photos until she found the post-pigeon-debacle picture on her laptop.

'Look, she's there, in your face…an ancient, wise old energy…' But I had to tell her that, to me, I just looked like the same old me.

'Here, read this.' Vassa handed me a hardback file with a white plastic cover. 'I don't let many people look at this stuff. You can take it away with you to study.'

Before we took our leave, Vassa fetched her *opele* and divining tray and the three of us sat around a table while she did a Life Path reading for Sally, which I recorded on my phone. That night, to Sally's chagrin, I accidentally blanked it.

The following day I decided to keep out of my sister's way. Suitably sun-blocked, I settled myself on a lounger under a black mangrove tree beside the swimming pool and opened Vassa's file.

The contents had been compiled by an assortment of Ifa priestesses – including Vassa – who were part of a secret, women-only society known as Nana Buuken. Immediately, I was hooked.

I learnt that Nana was one of the seven primordial female *orisha* who also went by the name of the *iyamis* or the Mothers – representing the primal female energies that had existed since the beginning of time. Oshun (she gets in everywhere) was, apparently, the leader of the *iyamis*. Nana was the oldest; she pre-dated the Iron Age, and to prove it she carried a knife made of bamboo.

I remembered how I'd had my first experience of the *iyamis* on our initial visit to Ola Olu, when Vassa invoked these energies to put a stop to young men in our family dying tragically early.

On a darker note, I learnt that if these healers and protectors of female interests were not given the respect and honour they deserved, their anger could be nuclear. As a force, they existed to see that justice was done, and to help them maintain balance and order in the universe, they'd been given the power to destroy as well as to create. In essence, the *iyamis* had been allocated the role of karma police, doling out, where appropriate, both punishment and reward. But above and beyond everything, their task was to protect and empower women.

I looked up from Vassa's file and around the Lilo-infested swimming pool; no men were about that day. A heavily made-up woman wearing headphones was lounging awkwardly on a turquoise dolphin; a Cuban teenager sat painting her nails on an acid-house-orange smiley. In the shallow end, a corpulent septuagenarian was leaning against the steps, reading a glossy magazine, as an uncannily skinny woman, her hair in a tight bun, schlepped from side-to-side of the pool, her eyes half-closed, in a walking meditation. Their passivity irked me. Thinking we could do with a bit of primordial *iyami* energy to shake things up, I dived into the water. Bland, surprised looks greeted me, and a few irritated ones. As usual, I was the only person actually swimming in the pool, but my lengths were constantly interrupted by the width-walking woman and floaters on inflatables. After ten minutes I gave up and continued ploughing through the folder.

I was interested to learn that some Yoruba women still have their own secret *iyami* societies, which they exclusively control; the menfolk don't get a look-in. Although they're often given the 'witch' label, there's more to an *iyami* than to your common-or-garden witch. *Iyamis* possess what is known as *aje* – which loosely translates as psychic power. *Aje* is most commonly inherited from an ancestor, but is occasionally bequeathed by an *orisha*. These 'wise women' are healers, herbalists, spiritualists – midwives, even – and can tune into both *orisha* energy and spiritual energy. Some, apparently, even have the ability to shape-shift and astral travel.

Iyami societies really got it in the neck once Christian colonialism took hold; they almost became extinct. Islam, too, had a fierce witch-annihilating agenda. Those few brave enough to keep going were forced to operate underground. It wasn't until 1951 that the British government put a stop to the massacres in which any woman suspected of being associated with an *iyami* society, or of practising the ancient ways, was subjected to burning, stoning or beheading.

I returned from the pool to find Sally on the terrace sketching a lone egret perched on one leg beneath a palm tree. She looked up at me and smiled.

'Good news. Vassa's said she'll write up my Life Path and email it to me. She jotted down the binary symbols, remember.'

'That's kind of her.' I'd been forgiven my clumsiness.

'Got to the bottom of your ancestor witch, yet?'

'No, but I'm on it.'

The next day, over lunch in the tree house, I handed Vassa back her file. She talked about the glass ceiling many would-be *iyanifas*

still came up against in America and other diasporic countries. In the early days, she'd even had to battle it out with Phil.

While some *babalawos* in Africa had welcomed the opportunity, condoned by colonialists, to push their female counterparts aside and take the reins, most knew the importance Ifa placed on gender balance. In other countries, however, it was quite a different matter.

In the late twentieth century, when the news began to surface that women in Africa were being initiated as *iyanifas*, female practitioners from around the world, and Afro-Americans wanting to reclaim their spiritual legacy, headed to Yorubaland in droves to undergo initiation. But once they returned home many of the unreconstructed *babalawos* practising in their countries, mirroring the exclusively male role of the Catholic priest, refused to acknowledge their female counterparts. And it didn't stop there. In some countries, female *orisha* were given a doll-like makeover to suit certain chauvinistic male tastes. Oshun, the untameable, primordial force, was sometimes depicted as a big-boobed, fair-skinned Latino in a frilly dress.

Vassa and her fellow *iyanifas* in the Nana Buuken society were constantly challenging this lingering chauvinism. Nana Buuken was Vassa's 'baby' – her version of a secret *iyami* society. Their function, she believed, was not only to empower women with ancient energy and wisdom, but also to work as a force for global healing and good.

Nana herself had a special place in Vassa's life. I was shocked when she told me, how, as a child, horrific abuse had been part of her day-to-day existence. Her life, Vassa claimed, was unbearable – until one night a white, tissue-like female shape came into her bedroom, and began stroking her hair, reassuring her that she would always be there to help her through her suffering.

'That vision's never left me,' said Vassa, with tears in her eyes.

'From that point on I've felt cared for…embraced…'

'Is she a kind of guardian angel?'

'More like a protective mother… I did some crazy stuff as a teenager, but she's always been there.'

'You're a survivor, Vassa.'

'Me? No. I call myself a thriver!'

'A thriver? That's good. I like that.'

'Nana corrects the DNA in your life – heals your body, mind, spirit. She sees everything.' Looking me in the eyes, Vassa added, 'You should train yourself to be open to that frequency.'

We were moving on, finally, to my ancestor witch. Somehow, I couldn't take her seriously. Perhaps I didn't want to. Ifa believes our ancestors incarnate through us. If that *was* the case, this very ancient female energy would have been hanging around for a long, long time.

Gator Jaw

KELLY, Ola Olu's Afro-American gardener, was busy pruning the bushes and hacking away at the undergrowth when we arrived for another day of rituals. While Vassa went up to the tree house to change, we chatted to him. I'd assumed he was an Ifa follower, too, and was surprised to discover he was actually an evangelical Christian.

Vassa emerged ten minutes later in a red Tyrolean hat and wellies, looking as if she was about to climb the Alps. As she came closer I noticed she was carrying a knife, and that the feather in her hat looked like an eagle's. Attached to the back of the hat was a small alligator tail.

'You guys have some deep shit,' she said, by way of explanation. 'This hat's for my protection.' She held out the knife for us to admire.

'Made from 'gator jaw.'

Sally had told her about a traditional healer, innocuously named Mama Precious, whom she'd consulted in Nigeria when she'd begun to feel unwell. Mama Precious rubbed herbs on her stomach, but all Sally experienced was excruciating pain. She said it felt like a dagger had been plunged into her and something had been punctured. Mama Precious claimed she was pulling out negative energy, but Sally was later diagnosed with a hiatus hernia. Careful to avoid the words *bad juju*, Vassa, nevertheless, reckoned something sinister had gone on in there and was determined to 'clear it out'. Sally herself was keen to release whatever it was that was blocking her from enjoying a truly nurturing partner-relationship in her life.

Vassa led her to a human-sized, metallic structure resembling an ornamental Victorian bird cage.

'This is the Bell,' she said. 'I want you to stand inside it, Sally. Stretch out your right arm and keep walking around and around in a circle.'

'I feel heavy, so, so heavy,' groaned Sally, several minutes later, already looking hot, dizzy and exhausted.

I sat down on a nearby bench to watch the spectacle – not, I'm ashamed to say, without a smidgen of *shadenfreude*.

Vassa warned her that she'd shortly be expected to do a lot of yelling, and asked her if she minded my being there. Sally responded that she'd rather I made myself scarce.

'We're English,' she panted. 'Easily embarrassed.'

I stood up, planning to relocate to another part of the gardens and read my Kindle, but I wasn't allowed to get off that lightly.

'You're coming with me,' said Vassa, marching me to the shrine of Ogun, the god of metal. 'You've got more shedding to do.' She lit a couple of sage sticks, handed me a rusty-looking machete, and instructed me to hold it out at arms' length, swing it to my left and to my right and 'slice out' all the crap in my life. Could there really be much more? The machete was heavy, and before long my arms started aching and I was horribly hot. In the distance I could hear Vassa yelling at Sally: 'Louder! Louder!... I can't hear you. Give it more!... Stab that knife into the ground! That's it. Stab it, plunge it into the earth!' Sally began yelling too. It sounded like a primal scream therapy session. I wondered what Kelly made of it all.

I, meanwhile, was battling to keep going, and felt ridiculous. I was so busy asking myself what the hell I was doing there and for what, that I forgot all about the shedding part. Why was Vassa spending so long with Sally and ignoring me? The more I swung, the angrier my thoughts became: I came here to connect with the love goddess, Oshun, and perform her rituals, not swing a bloody weapon around in this jungle while my sister stabbed a 'gator jaw into the ground. But the stubborn part of me carried on swinging the machete, determined to see it through – whatever 'it' was.

Quite abruptly, the yelling stopped. Silence reigned. A few minutes later I glanced over my shoulder and saw that Sally was now curled up in a foetal position on the lap of the shrine of the nurturing *orisha*, Omilade – a twenty-five-foot-long, rather beautiful sculpture of a horizontal mermaid figure, covered in mosaics and sea shells. Ogun's ugly metal face stared back at me. Nestled beneath Omilade's ample bosom, with the sun shining on her face, Sally looked beatific. As for Vassa, she was nowhere to be seen. Rage flared up inside me; I'd been abandoned.

Then I spied Vassa several metres away. But she wasn't coming over to rescue me. Kelly was at her side. She was telling him what she wanted him to do with a clump of messy palms. That did it. I dropped the machete and called her over.

She took one look at my face. 'You're really pissed at me, aren't you?'

'Is it good Ifa practice,' I asked, through gritted teeth, 'to set up a ritual like this and then just bugger off? Or did you forget about me?'

'Come with me, Diane.'

She led me to the healing matrix of the seven mothers; the glade of tall trees where the primordial mothers, the *iyamis,* resided. I liked this peaceful spot, close to Oshun's shrine, where patterned gourds dangled from branches. A washstand and a bowl of water had been placed in the centre of the glade.

'This water,' said Vassa, picking up a jug, 'contains medicinal leaves, herbs and a meteor rock which I've exposed to the full moon.'

She proceeded to pour the water, which smelt of mint and lemon, all over my head and then to rub in *Ifa Ose* – the purifying African black soap. The water was deliciously cool and soothing. A gentle breeze sprang up in the glade, as it had previously, and the wind chimes began to tinkle.

'Ah, here they come,' said Vassa, as she gently massaged my scalp. My head was bent over the washstand and my eyes were closed to keep out the soap, so I couldn't see who 'they' were – but I could hear their *caw caw caw* squawk as they flapped about above me.

'They're circling around you, Diane. I'm counting them. Yes, there are seven. Seven crows for the seven *iyamis.* They've come to heal you.'

It was then, as the *iyamis* flew around me, that I understood my rage. As a psychotherapist I'm pretty good at being able to fathom other people's conscious and unconscious triggers, but that doesn't necessarily mean that I find it easy to get in touch with my own. My rage was buried. I'd been very close to my mother until little sister Sally came along, and for an assortment of painful reasons, none of which were Sally's fault, I experienced feelings of abandonment. My relationship with my mother began to fall apart, and didn't properly heal until I began practising Buddhism twenty or so years later. Witnessing my sister being the sole recipient of Vassa's attention, and then seeing her curled up in the lap of the motherly Omilade, mirrored those historic emotions of being left out in the cold.

'OK, I get it,' I said, drying my hair on the towel Vassa had just handed me. 'Thanks.' She smiled. I didn't need to say any more. She'd known all along what it was I'd needed to shed.

Still reeling from the day's rituals, my sister and I meandered alongside the shoreline of the Atlantic Ocean. The swim we'd hoped for in the alluring astral twilight was sadly out of the question; the sea was too wild. Sally was flying home in the morning and neither of us were too happy about it.

'This *orisha* stuff is certainly powerful.' Sally gave me a worried look. 'And you've still got all your Oshun rituals to come.'

'Yeah, I'm having mixed feelings about having to process all this bizarre material on my own.'

'You can WhatsApp me.'

'Thanks. I will.'

We stopped to look at what we thought was a shark, but it was only a piece of driftwood being battered by the waves.

Sally turned to look at me. 'So where do *you* think all this sits with our Buddhist practice?'

'I've struggled with that a bit,' I confessed, 'but here's what I reckon...' I took a deep breath. 'Buddhist writings are scattered with references to gods, goddesses and universal energies...'

I paused as a huge wave crashed against the shore.

'Isn't Ifa's big 'God' – Olodumare – genderless, too, like the Mystic Law in Buddhism?' Sally added.

'Yes. Ifa has quite a bit in common with Buddhism – besides

reincarnation.'

Sally took out her iPhone. I assumed, at first, that she was looking at her messages, but a few moments later she read out a passage from The Nirvana Sutra:

All scriptures or teachings, from whatever source, are ultimately the revelation of Buddhist truth. They are not non-Buddhist teachings.

She looked up at me. 'I guess that means Ifa is a part of the unfathomable Mystic Law...along with everything else.'

'I see it this way: that bit of old driftwood floating over there, and the diamonds they scoop up from the sea bed off the coast of Namibia are both contained within the waters of this immense Atlantic Ocean...'

Sally yawned. 'It's getting dark. How about the farewell drink you've been promising me?

'Yeah. Let's go to that Cuban bar and listen to some salsa.'

Hurricane Hermine

SALLY WAS back in England; Vassa had gone to ground. Tranquillity reigned in my little patch of the planet. But not for long.

One morning I wandered over to the villa-complex reception desk to ask for more dishwasher powder, and overheard a family of Dutch tourists asking if they could rent a villa for a few days to shelter from the hurricane.

'What hurricane?' I asked the nervous-looking receptionist. He stared at me as if I'd just crawled out of a Borneo jungle after fifty years.

'You mean you haven't heard?'

'I've steered clear of the news for the last couple of days. Isn't that what being on holiday's all about?'

'Well, Hermine's coming our way tonight. Got enough food, Ma'am? You're gonna have to hunker down for a day or three.'

'Wasn't this supposed to be the sunshine state?'

'We haven't had a hurricane since Wilma, eleven years ago now. I guess you're just unlucky.'

'Guess I am.'

I walked back to the villa cursing. Why were hurricanes given such innocuous old-lady names, like Hermine and Wilma? They should be called Bruce or Butch. Strong winds have always unsettled me. Now that I was more *orisha*-savvy, I could point the finger at Oya, that ferocious warrior-goddess of wind and transformation, who blasts her way through oceans, continents and lives, destroying whatever or whoever happens to be in her path.

Clutching the TV remote control, I scrolled through countless channels until I found a local one. A spokeswoman for County Emergency Management was warning that Hermine was a Category One hurricane: schools and offices were to remain closed and we were to expect dangerous wind speeds, downed trees and power outages. She advised us to secure the exterior of our homes, check for weak branches on trees and make sure we were equipped with supplies such as food, water and medicine.

I looked out the window. The sky was darkening even though it was still the afternoon, and the fridge was just about empty. The nearest shop was in a gas station a twenty-minute bike ride away. I cycled to it, hell for leather. The shop had little enough stock at the best of times, and I wasn't the only one panic-buying. The bread and milk had all gone, but there was pasta aplenty and peanut butter and Hershey bars. I reckoned a hurricane was a good enough excuse to hit the carbs.

I stayed glued to a Florida news channel until the early hours of the morning. At one point Florida Governor Rick Scott came on and urged residents to move inland before Hermine hit land. But I eventually tired of apocalyptic voices and countless fingers pointing at swarms of arrows on rolling weather maps, and, with earplugs firmly inserted, took myself off to bed and prayed that I wouldn't wake up in the Atlantic Ocean or the Gulf of Mexico.

Well, I survived Hermine. She was a bit of a disappointment, actually; no roofless villas, broken power lines or felled trees – at least none that I could see through the window the following morning; only masses of leaves, flower-heads, trash everywhere and a few broken branches. Many others in the state weren't so lucky, though.

I was still housebound, thanks to the torrential rain which had appeared in the hurricane's wake; this deluge beat every monsoon I'd ever witnessed. But it provided some entertainment, too: frogs and toads hopped around outside and the pond carp were leaping higher than ever. A giant turtle appeared from time to time and tapped his foot on the glass door as if he were asking for shelter.

Folks back home had seen the news reports about the hurricane and I received worried messages, but the person I expected to be the most concerned about my safety – my partner – appeared blithely unconcerned. Fuelling my irritation, I discovered David was on the Lofoten Islands in the Arctic having the time of his life. Warmed by the Gulf Stream, the temperatures there were in the seventies. While I attempted to get to grips with cabin fever and alcohol drought, he sent me photos of blue skies, gorgeous, deserted, white sand beaches and mountains rising out of the sea. One smug *see what you're missing, LOL* selfie really irked me. Taken at 7pm, he was sitting shirtless, in glorious sunshine, raising a glass of Ricard. Grrr.

When the rain finally stopped, I hopped onto my bike and cycled to an out-of-the-way riverside spot with my camera.

On an earlier ride I'd noticed a multitude of different-coloured butterflies hovering over a certain clump of bushes, and wanted to take a few shots of them.

I was busy clicking away when I noticed a heavily-bearded guy in a baseball cap on the far side of the cycle track, grinning menacingly at me while doing on-the-spot jogger exercise. He waved and started walking towards me. My rapist-radar bleeped. I jumped back on the bike and cycled off.

An hour later, I returned to the same spot to finish photographing the butterflies. Stupid, I know.

'You sure are a pretty gal,' he called out, as he crept up behind me, thrusting out his hand – which I had little choice but to shake. It was the nicest compliment I'd received for some time – just a shame it had to come from a blank-eyed, wilderness weirdo who looked considerably brawnier than I am. A cross-examination followed: Where was I from? How long was I over for? Had I come on my own? Where was I staying? I was trapped between him and the river. Adrenaline hormones surged through me, triggering a fight-or-flight response, increasing my perspiratory, respiratory and heart rates, but also improving my vision: I saw something long, black and familiar dart across the bike path a few feet away and slither into the undergrowth.

'A snake! A snake!' I yelled. His attention momentarily distracted, I darted off, leapt onto my bike and pedalled away at the speed of lightning.

Back at the villa I added *black* to my Google search for *Snakes of Florida* and discovered that there were only two of them. My reptilian rescuer must have been either a Black Racer or an Indigo snake.

I like to think this one was an Indigo snake.

San Agustín

AFTER FOUR days of solitude, Vassa scooped me up for a day of sightseeing. Temperatures had soared. We stopped to buy pots of frozen yogurt to eat as we drove along the highway.

I was thinking how pleasant it was to spend friend/friend rather than priestess/acolyte time in Vassa's company when her car phone rang.

A guy with a dry mouth whispered in a panicky voice that he needed to speak with Vassa immediately; it was an emergency.

'OK, go ahead, Gene,' said Vassa, licking her spoon.

'A police car's parked up at the end of my drive… I want you to do a reading for me, Vassa.'

Although we hadn't met, I'd seen Gene's photo and knew a bit about him already. Part Cuban, he was a handsome, dark-haired, bandana-wearing, tattooed guy of around thirty-five. Based in Florida, he organised *ayahuasca* tea parties all over the States. Also known as 'The Spirit Molecule', *ayahuasca* is a hallucinogenic substance that contains a powerful psychoactive

174

molecule. Those who regularly ingest it claim it cleanses the body and the spirit, and can cure addictions and depression. It's also known to trigger nightmarish, psychotic episodes.

'He's a guy with real integrity… Gene's turned his life around and now he's trying to help people,' Vassa explained. 'Some of his clients are very rich and want to get off drugs.'

Gene sent the *ayahuasca* clients he reckoned were in need of further healing on to Vassa, and made use of her divination services himself. His current predicament had come about due to earlier clashes with the police. At twenty, he'd been done for drug possession, and later for a car violation – after which he was warned by the courts that a third offence, however minor, would land him a five to seven-year prison sentence. This Sword of Damocles had been dangling over his head for years, and as he talked more about his precarious situation it seemed likely that it was finally about to drop.

A condition for taking *ayahuasca* is that participants in the tea party are totally drug-free – and that means all drugs – not just those that get you high. Shamans in the Peruvian rainforest who conduct *ayahuasca* ceremonies for westerners even go as far as banning anti-malarial medication. The present crisis had come about because at one of Gene's recent tea parties a participant who had declared himself drug-free went on to have a fit after drinking the tea. Gene rushed him to hospital, where he learned that the man was on anti-depressant medication and Xanax – an anti-anxiety sedative. The police were called to the hospital and the patient was interviewed.

Gene was breathless and close to tears. 'Not only that, Vassa, I'm pretty sure my ex has talked to the police, too. I'm shot. They're gonna send me down.'

I was feeling anxious for Gene. Vassa, however, continued to eat her yogurt and navigate the traffic. How the hell did she stay so cool?

'I can't do a reading for you, honey; I'm in the car with Diane – I'm taking her to St Augustine.'

'But Vassa, the police officer who was in the hospital, he's parked up outside…'

'What are you doing about your fear, Gene?'

'I've put my machete on the drive.'

'That's good.' Vassa turned to me. 'He's an Ogun, too.'

'I'm going to Colombia before they arrest me,' said Gene. 'I've got a friend there. I can't do time.'

Vassa's tone was soothing. 'Walk your dog, as usual. I'll do a reading for you when I get back home.'

She hung up and gave me a rueful smile. 'I'm so sad for Gene. *Ayahuasca* is *almost* legal here. There's only one ingredient they still need to clear.'

The Bridge of Lions, which impressively straddles a mammoth estuary, signalled our approach to the city of St Augustine. The city felt so weirdly un-American that for a few moments I wondered if I'd been given a psychoactive substance, too. The architecture dictated that I ought to be in Spain or Latin America. I've never visited anywhere in the States that has such a historic vibe. I later discovered that the city was founded in 1585 by the Spanish admiral Pedro Menéndez de Avilés, who named the settlement San Agustín. Shiploads of Spanish settlers and soldiers soon piled in, and for over 200 years this became the capital of Spanish Florida.

The old town was a delightful mishmash of colonial buildings, antiquated, wooden houses and ponies and traps. Fountains and sculptures almost out-numbered the palm trees. Petunias, redbuds, orchids, violets, and azaleas – I lost count of the arrays of flowers growing in well-tended beds and hanging baskets dangling above doorways. The city was awash with sunshine and colour, but somehow Gene's situation put a pall over it all; I was back at work in my clinic, worrying about a distraught client.

Vassa's phone rang. It was Gene again. The police officer had turned his car around in the drive and driven away. She looked pleased: Ogun had sent him packing. The emergency was over for the time being, but Gene still wanted a reading to determine whether he should head off to Colombia.

We continued to wander the streets of the city. I had to content myself with admiring the fortress of Castillo de San Marcos at a distance, as Vassa refused to go inside.

'It's truly haunted,' she explained. And this was a woman who had spent her life wrestling with otherworldly, unwieldy *orisha*. Perhaps she wasn't as tough as I'd thought.

The impressive-looking fort had been constructed to protect the civilians of San Agustín from my hostile countrymen. When we Brits were fighting the Spanish, Sir Francis Drake sacked and burnt the city. Eighty years later, Robert Searle, an English pirate, sacked and burnt it again, ransoming off hostages and selling others into slavery. Mariana, the Spanish Queen Regent, wisely ordered the construction of a fire-proof fortress. Although the British made two further attempts at besieging the city, they were unable to penetrate the walls of the Castillo de San Marcos. Florida became a British colony in 1763 and during the War of Independence the fort served as a military prison. The fledgling US government went on to use San Marcos as a prison for Native Americans.

'Just think,' said Vassa, with a shudder, 'all the spirits of all those people who were tortured and killed over centuries are still inside those castle walls...'

Our conversation about psychoactive drugs continued on the drive back. Although they're viewed as sacred by some West African animist religions, I hadn't come across any references in Ifa to their usage. Vassa was friendly with a young woman who travelled the world holding hallucinogenic parties for the rich and famous. The substance she gave them to ingest came from the backs of toads – not any old toad – only the Cane Toad. They didn't lick the toad's actual back (dogs known to have made that mistake have come a cropper). The 'magic' secretion, 5-methoxy-N, N-dimethyltryptamine, releases tons of feel-good chemicals into the body, along with hallucinations. The hit, which only lasts a few minutes, is, apparently, very powerful. Vassa mentioned the names of a couple of celebrities and billionaires – including a Saudi sheik and his model girlfriend – who lived from one 'party' to another. Like Gene, the young woman in question sent her casualties to Vassa for an *orisha* fix. The 'toad lady' wanted Phil and Vassa to go into business with her but they refused. Vassa said she continued to advise her on 'moral issues'.

Back at the house, I took myself off for a shower while Vassa did a reading for Gene over the phone. When I came out of the shower room her smile has vanished.

'It's looking really bad for him. Unless he can change something in his life, he's gonna have to go to Colombia…'

'But that seems so drastic…'

'All the effort he's put into building his business up – he'll be leaving everything behind, including US citizenship.'

That evening Phil invited us for a meal in a Japanese restaurant. Vassa, for once, was quiet, and though she tried her best to hide it, preoccupied. Phil picked at his sushi, bemused by the whole Gene story. He wondered, as did I, why he even risked holding his tea parties when a potential jail sentence hung over him.

Washington Oaks

Ok, so I'd seen evidence of Adunni's legacy in the States, and how Ifa was carving out a niche for itself there, but apart from a spine tingle at Ola Olu when I'd first placed an offering at Oshun's shrine by the lake, I still hadn't succeeded in getting any closer to the goddess herself. This, however, was about to change.

Vassa was late. I'd been waiting for her in a quiet spot close to the entrance of the villa complex – out of earshot of my noisy new neighbours from Kentucky – for half an hour. Suddenly a cacophony of *caw, caw, cawing* started up. Nestling in the giant sycamore trees above me I could see the ornithological equivalent of my Kentuckian neighbours – a massive flock of rambunctious crows.

The hoard of Kentuckians – their ages ranging from eight to eighty – had moved in a couple of days earlier, with masses of their own bedding and crate upon crate of beer. Only so many guests were allowed per villa. I'd lost count of this lot. I could have reported them but I'm not that type of person – not to say that I hadn't been sorely tempted. My main objection was that they seemed incapable of holding a normally-pitched conversation, and spent most of the day on their veranda drinking, shouting at one another and playing bluegrass and heavy metal music at full-volume.

'You're here at last!' I yelled, as Vassa pulled up beside me in the Fiat. 'These crows are driving me crazy.'

Vassa gave a knowing laugh. 'They're looking out for you.'

As we drove along the highway I told her about my neighbours, and how the racket they were making had driven the koi carp away from my pond. According to Gee, the manager, this was their breeding ground and home. Soon after the rabble arrived, the fish disappeared under the bridge, en masse, into another section of the estate's waterway. I missed their magnificent colouration and calming presence. When my sister and I chanted together on the terrace they leapt joyfully about the pond.

Carp are known for their well-developed hearing. They sense sound through their ears, and through a vertebral system that transfers vibrations from what is known as their swim bladder – the fish version of a hearing aid – to their inner ear. Carp, like myself, must be more into Buddhist chanting than heavy metal.

'Don't worry,' Vassa reassured me, 'you'll be seeing more carp today. I was late because I had to buy hermit crabs.'

'Hermit crabs, why?'

'Your offering for Oshun.'

I looked around. Sitting on the back seat was a transparent container with tiny crabs floating about inside. I wasn't sure if they were dead or alive; nor was I in the mood to ask.

'Where are you taking me?'
'Washington Oaks.'

Washington Oaks Gardens State Park is located on a barrier island nestling between the Atlantic Ocean to the east and the Matanzas River to the west. Native Americans had once hunted and fished there – and so had a surveyor called George Washington, (a relative of the American president of the same name), who, at one time, owned the land.

Vassa handed me the crabs and led me through exotic gardens and citrus groves to the wide estuary-river which flows through the park. At the river's edge I was instructed to take each of the twelve crabs, one by one, cradle them in my cupped palms, say a prayer to Oshun and then release them into the water. The sun was directly overhead. I'd come without a hat and my head was starting to ache. While Vassa recited the opening prayer in Yoruba, I took a good look at these decapod crustaceans. Close up, I could see they were alive, kicking and dying to get free.

Hermit crabs, like crows, are scavengers. But it isn't food they scavenge for, its gastropod shells. These poor, unprotected crustaceans lack a shell of their own and have to go in search of a discarded one. I guess it's like living in a house without a roof. When shells are scarce hermit crabs fight over them; during a shell famine they've been known to use substitutes such as empty Coke cans, flower pots and even pieces of Lego.

In addition to feeling hot and irritable, I now felt nervous. The shell-less little creatures looked so vulnerable in my hand. It wasn't their tiny pincers I was afraid of but that there might be a repeat of the pigeon fiasco at Ola Olu and I'd end up making an idiot of myself again. I couldn't, at that moment, think of twelve things to pray about either, and would have preferred to chuck the crabs straight into the river and jump in after them to cool off. A crab running up and down your arm was mightily distracting when you're trying to come up with twelve different prayers. But, like a good Girl Guide, I did my best.

Once the twelfth crab had rejoined its natural habitat something changed. The breeze lifted. Little waves began to lap against the river bank. My mood shifted too, and so did my headache. A carp-like calm descended upon me. Vassa, on the other hand, became fired up.

'See, she's getting it! She's getting it! She's sending you a sign!'

Then, a most extraordinary thing happened: a pair of dolphins swam leisurely past us. This was the first time I'd seen dolphins in the wild. I was immensely excited.

'Oshun's sending you joy!' Vassa clapped her hands. And I did feel joyful. My spine tingled. I sensed a benign presence hovering around me – thrilling yet unnerving. For the first time in Florida I felt truly touched, once again, by Oshun.

A good-looking man in shorts and a boater paddled past and smiled at us; perched in the helm of the canoe was a cute-looking puppy.

'There. She's sending you one of those, too.'

'Guy, canoe or puppy?'

'You've got yourself a guy. A little puppy would make you happy. A canoe sure would, too.'

Vassa suggested I pick up a few shells as an Oshun keepsake. For the first time I noticed all the coquina shells lining the river bank. I offered to pay Vassa for the crabs, but she wouldn't hear of it.

'Save your coins for the carp pond,' she said. 'Let's go.'

We loitered in the rose garden. The atmosphere seemed heightened. I loved smelling the roses that actually smelt of roses. I felt alive and connected. Twice now, I reflected, I've been 'touched' by Oshun: while splashing my face in the Oshun River years ago, and just now beside the Matanzas River. The first time she was completely unexpected, and even though I came to Florida actively looking for her, she'd managed, once again, to take me by surprise. What had I felt beside the Matanzas River? A presence, yes, and an energy swirling around me; an elevated mood; joy; connection; followed by a sense of feeling somehow lighthearted and healed.

We continued our walk alongside exquisite beds of azaleas, camellias and bird of paradise blooming in the shade of magnolia trees, until we reached the centrepiece of the park – a magnificent, towering oak estimated to be around 300 years old.

'Did you know,' I asked Vassa, pleased, for once, to have the opportunity to share some arcane knowledge of my own, 'that the word druid comes from the Gaelic word *diur* meaning oak tree?'

'Those druids were pretty cool people; it doesn't surprise me.'

'They didn't use cowrie shells or *opeles* for divination, they used the oak.'

'That figures.'

We chatted about the recent discovery by arboreal researchers that trees communicated with each other via complex networks of fungi, which they'd christened the wood-wide web.

'Yeah.' Vassa picked up an acorn and put it in her pocket. 'They're saying forests are like human families. Parent trees support their sapling kids.'

'And healthy trees,' I added, 'share their nutrients with neighbours that are undernourished or sick.'

Vassa's eyes lit up. 'I so wish you could meet John! He comes over from Australia every year with his didgeridoo and plays to all the trees in Ola Olu.'

'I wish I could meet John, too.'

'It's incredible, the difference that wonderful sound makes to the health of our trees. He goes up, down and around them, and does the same with any people who are hanging out in the gardens… What a feeling!'

We finally reached the carp ponds only to discover they'd been roped off and were being drained 'for maintenance purposes'. There wasn't a koi to be seen. Disappointed, I returned my wishing-pond coins to my purse.

Back at the villa, I poured myself an ice-cold Bud Light and ventured out onto the terrace. Peace reigned. The Kentuckians had left. The carp, hadn't, as yet, returned to the pond, but I felt sure they would.

The day had affirmed something of importance for me: She wasn't a figment of my imagination. I was now certain that this energy known as Oshun definitely existed.

Natura

I'VE ALWAYS felt close to nature, but in Florida I became hypersensitive to it; I soaked it up keenly, everywhere, every day. Walking alongside the river one evening I heard a splashing beneath me. I looked down; a family of manatees were lumbering past in the shallows. These ungraceful yet loveable creatures are prolific in the waterways of Florida. Also known as sea cows, with their greyish, wrinkled, leathery skin, manatees are more like the elephants they're believed to be distantly related to. Their clumsiness and genial ugliness made me laugh.

I didn't have to go looking for any of the creatures that I seemed to be crossing paths with on a daily basis – be they vultures, snakes, turtles, manatees, dolphins or the crows that sometimes circled above me; somehow they'd become part of my habitat. Did this, I wonder, have anything to do with the rituals I'd been participating in?

Goddesses the world over, Oshun included, have had strong associations with the natural world. A hundred years ago, the

British Egyptologist, Margaret Murray, claimed that an old religion, based around an ancient fertility cult that celebrated nature, had flourished in Britain and Europe until it was stamped out by Christianity. Devotees feasted, danced, held magical ceremonies, performed ritual copulation and worshipped the Great Mother. The more spiritually inclined supporters of the women's movement, later in the century, leapt upon Murray's claims as evidence that a predominantly matriarchal culture had once existed. In recent years, Murray's largely unsubstantiated research has been discredited by academics unable to find evidence to support her theory of an organised goddess cult in Europe. But that hasn't been enough to dissuade the faithful from performing goddess and nature-veneration rituals – often alongside an assortment of New Age practices.

According to Jung, the powerful archetype of the Great Mother, who contains the dual aspect of creation and destruction, is buried deep in our collective global psyche. She is the personification of the feminine principle, and represents the fertile womb out of which all life comes; Mother Nature in the primordial swamp where life is being constantly spawned and constantly devoured.

Nature-goddess worship is fairly ubiquitous, although in many Christian and Muslim societies it's synonymous with witchcraft. This is hardly surprising, given the imbalance, perversity and fear of female power inherent in patriarchal religions. Recent research, however, indicates that not only did Jesus have female disciples – a couple of whom even bankrolled him – but women also held positions of power in the Church, until, between the 4th and 7th centuries, the likes of testosterone-fuelled Roman emperor Constantine, a Christian convert, and an assortment of misogynistic popes, airbrushed them out of history.

The Great Mother of this ancient European religion and

Jung's universal archetype appear to have much in common with Ifa's Nana Buuken, the oldest primal female energy that has existed since the beginning of time. She's also one of the *iyamis* – the primordial energies of which Oshun is the leader. And *iyamis* – at least those in the trees at Ola Olu – apparently like to shapeshift into crows. From the Middle Ages onwards, in many European countries, crows were vilified as the witch's 'familiar' – aiding and abetting her in her malevolent curses and spells. Celtic goddesses were believed to gather over battlefields in the form of crows or ravens, and feed on the flesh of fallen warriors. But within Ifa, as practised in Africa, they're praised as the protectors of women; the embodiment of the *iyamis*.

Goddesses, traditionally, have high priestesses. Within Ifa they go by the name of *iyanifas*. In the tarot, the High Priestess is possibly the most enigmatic card in the major arcana. She symbolises the mysterious female principle; the guardian of the secret inner realms of the unconscious.

High priestesses – Adunni and Vassa being prime examples – are usually powerful, creative women in their own right. The first named author in the history of writing, Enheduanna, was a high priestess – and a clever one at that. She lived 4,000 years ago in the city of Ur, in what is now southern Iraq, and wrote beautiful poems in praise of the goddess Inanna, a powerful female deity.

In most cases it would appear that the decision to be initiated as a priestess comes about after experiencing an overwhelming sense of affinity with the deity in question, and a desire, on the part of the devotee, to take on her attributes and qualities. But others, like Adunni, are cherry-picked by that divinity – who sometimes, for brief periods, deigns to inhabit them. The subject arose one morning when she and I were on our way to the Sacred Groves.

'I didn't go looking for Oshun. She found me,' Adunni sighed. I'd asked her how long it had taken her to become initiated as a fully-fledged high priestess of *orisha*.

'Ten years,' she'd replied, winding down the window, thereby rendering the air-con ineffective and letting in flies. 'Ten very long years – but invigorating years all the same.'

'What is it you actually do in these rituals, if you don't mind me asking?'

'As a high priestess, one of my tasks is the construction of an *ebo*, which I will be doing today to place in Oshun's shrine.'

'You'll probably think this is a silly question, but why, exactly, do you perform these rituals?'

'I perform rituals to intensify my powers.'

I could detect in her voice that she was tired of being asked questions by journalists, cultural tourists and the likes of me.

'How do you go about constructing this *ebo*?'

'I gather ingredients from nature, which together symbolise and radiate the psychic essence of the universe.'

'What sort of ingredients?'

'Plants, feathers, fur, stones, shells, bones, minerals and so on…'

I smiled. 'No wonder your bag is so heavy!'

'It precedes my mystic transformation into goddess.'

I was curious to know how long this mystic transformation lasted. Adunni shrugged her shoulders. 'That depends on Oshun. Only a few very powerful priests and priestesses can represent *orisha* all the time.'

'So the primary calling of a high priestess is to serve her goddess?'

Adunni turned to me. 'It is also her sacred duty to assert and reassert the divinity of humankind.'

Woman of Wisdom

I WAS KEEN to further explore the connection between Oshun and the Great Mother and the calling to become a high priestess of Ifa. I'd met a couple of African Ifa priestesses in Nigeria, years ago, but the two I'd had the most connection with were white. It was time, I decided, to have a chat with a black *iyanifa*.

I hit the jackpot when I found her; not only was Ayele Kumari, PhD, a fully-fledged African American *iyanifa*, she was also the author of a book entitled *Iyanifa: Woman of Wisdom*. Ayele's book consists of interviews with an assortment of priestesses who practise both 'African' Ifa and 'diasporic' Ifa.

Ayele agreed to let me interview her, and we connected over Zoom. She was a warm, fulsome lady, with a deep voice and an infectious laugh, and emblazoned on the wall of her Missouri home was an African tapestry. Behind her, I could see an assortment of African carvings.

ME: Thanks for agreeing to this interview, Ayele. Let's start at the beginning. When did you first hear about Ifa?

AYELE: I first heard about it through a reading I had in 1992. So I knew it was around but I wasn't gravitating towards it. I thought my path lay elsewhere. I was a college professor. I taught biology, anatomy and physiology. I'd supervised around 7,000 students.

ME: Can you tell me about your calling to initiation?

AYELE: Sure. Ifa changed my life drastically. I woke up one morning at 3am and literally could not walk. I had to crawl to the restroom. I ended up in hospital.

ME: What was wrong?

AYELE: The doctors couldn't find anything wrong, but I had a dream that week in hospital that I was at a *babalawo*'s home and he needed to share some secret technology with me. I started dreaming that my life was going to change – it was quite frightening. I managed to trace this *babalawo* and tell him I was in hospital and that I'd had a dream about him.

ME: What was his reaction?

AYELE: He did a reading and said I was called to initiate and might not walk until I did. It was pretty scary. What? How? Why? But I knew people were called to Ifa through an illness. I agreed to initiate and everything fell into place.

ME: How, exactly?

AYELE: Within a month I was in Miami undergoing the rites, and I was walking again a month later. Still, I didn't understand, didn't know why it had to be that way. But my ancestors came and told me I'd done this six times before [been an *iyanifa*] and this was my seventh time – that I'd agreed to this before coming here [her current incarnation]. This helped me to accept my path, but I still didn't know what it would look like.

ME: How did it change your life?

AYELE: Every aspect changed. My mother got sick and I had to give up my job and become a full-time care-giver. At the same time as caring, I did the Ifa training.

ME: I understand you work as a healer these days.

AYELE: Yes, I'm a healer and a diviner. Most of the people come to me for some aspect of healing; some inner work always needs to be done. I've worked with people with cancer and with numerous conditions.

ME: And you use Ifa for this?

AYELE: Yes, Ifa plays a role. I balance out – I do the reading, get an idea of what's spiritually going on. I also bring holistic medicine to the table.

ME: What, if any, is your relationship with Oshun?

AYELE: I was initiated into Oya and Obatala, and after that into Oshun. You can initiate into multiple *orisha*. Each plays a different role for me. Oshun toned down the extreme of how Oya shows up.

ME: How?

AYELE: She brings more of the cowrie shell diviner – she wanted me to learn the shells – it gives me double energy. Oshun plays a big part in how I relate to the *iyami* and how I work with women. My work is centred around women and their empowerment.

ME: In the light of her prominent role in the Creation myth, and as leader of the *iyamis*, what do you think women can learn from Oshun?

AYELE: Empowerment. A lot of practitioners in the diaspora focus on her sensual aspect. But I think that Oshun was the first feminist. Feminism comes with stigma these days, and pre-conceived ideas. Oshun has spoken on behalf of women and women's power since the beginning of time, emphasising the power of the feminine and its role in Creation.

ME: Is there anything else women can learn from Oshun?

AYELE: Yes, we don't just need empowerment but also to show sisterhood. In her role she is bringing together the feminine energies – there were other primordial feminine forces around at the time of Creation. She brought them together, and in that role and in that way she teaches us sisterhood.

ME: Why do you think sisterhood matters?

AYELE: Practices that were unique to women have been usurped by men. There is a need for women to look at Odu Ifa and its translations from a woman's perspective, because when they do, sometimes the story changes significantly. We need to reclaim that which is ours. I feel that is what, ultimately, we can also learn from Oshun, and not be afraid to share. Oshun shares a lot with me in divination.

ME: What connection, if any, do you think Oshun has with the Great Mother?

AYELE: I've used the term Great Mother myself but it's layered. When compared to the European Great Mother, she could be considered as that, but as it relates to African traditions there tends to be more of a pantheon of Great Mother goddesses. And as it relates to the Odu Ose Otura [which recounts Oshun's seminal role in the creation myth] there are other 'Great Mothers' involved – Onile, for example, who is an earth goddess.

ME: Some people claim that Mami Wata has nothing to do with Oshun, yet others – including devotees in Oshogbo – say that it's another name for her. What are your thoughts on this?

AYELE: Oshun, being a water spirit from the river, is very much associated with Mami Wata. Much of my research has been about how women's traditions have shown up throughout the continent. Mami Wata refers to a pantheon of water spirits who exist throughout Africa and are particularly popular in Benin. Mami Wata appears in multiple ways but can be seen in the diaspora as one entity. Oshun is just as much Mami Wata as the other water spirits.

ME: When it comes to the issue of cultural appropriation, criticism has been levelled at both Suzanne Wenger and Iyanifa Vassa for practising an African belief system. What is your take on this?

AYELE: I can see both sides of the argument. When it comes to forces of nature – which is what we are dealing with here – they're not limited to Nigeria, they're not limited to Cuba. Nature exists throughout the entire planet. If a person's *ori* [spiritual destiny] has agreed that this is the path they need to walk prior to reaching earth then who are we to question that? It is what it is. With individual practitioners it's not so much of an issue.

ME: And the other side of the argument?

AYELE: I do understand the concern because what happens is that appropriation becomes systemically implemented, so that you end up having a situation where the whole tradition becomes abused. The challenge is when the cultural point gets lost, and many of the African traditions have been lost under the influence of other cultures.

ME: Which cultures are you thinking of?

AYELE: It's a challenge for people when it gets expressed through European voices – particularly in the diaspora, because many came to be where they are through the institution of slavery. They could be killed for practising their ancestral traditions. So these days, when they reach out towards their ancestral traditions, they're seeking them as means of healing their own spirits as well as their ancestral spirits and their generational history…

ME: Yes, of course…

AYELE: …and it's difficult to make the adjustment when you're trying to reconnect with that which was taken away to discover it now has to be filtered through the ones that enslaved you and your ancestors in the first place... So I can understand the political, sociological, psychological aspects of it, but as far as the ecological and spiritual aspects are concerned, it is what it is. But I think it would do us well to be sensitive to why certain things are as they are.

ME: And Suzanne Wenger?

AYELE: I've not heard many people have issue with Suzanne Wenger, although I'm sure they did at some point. Maybe through her life's experiences she has proven herself through her commitment just to live the culture – as opposed to going there, bringing it back, and then trying to change it or shape it in another way. She's honoured the walk and she's honoured the path as it was presented to her.

ME: My understanding was that from the beginning she followed the African tradition...

AYELE: Because of that I think she gains more acceptance. And also for her efforts in reviving Oshogbo and the energy of Oshogbo, which in many ways has led to it being a more stable place that many adherents can come to now. It's hard to say, but in some ways those that took away were also some of those that were able to save the last vestiges before it was totally eliminated, and have helped create the space for its resurgence into a new generation.

ME: How have you managed to navigate your way through the sometimes confusing and conflicting traditions of diasporic Ifa and African Ifa?

AYELE: It's very much a web. Ifa said Ifa is for the world, but we also have various cultural paradigms that show up. I am African American. I have eight generations on my mother's side here in the United States, so there are certain things that are unique to our culture that are different to being raised on the continent of Africa.

ME: So your perspective is essentially that of an African American?

AYELE: We all bring certain views to Ifa and it is a dance to try to maintain the traditional recherché view without losing some parts of ourselves. But I also try to find it within traditional African cultural systems of Odu Ifa and Ifa to build that bridge. That's led me to study the history of Nigeria, the history of West Africa and so on.

ME: Has it helped?

AYELE: The *ancient* African traditions, they help me to connect as an African American woman, and one who is very much interested in women's empowerment. When they say 'women can't do this', I say 'wait, wait, historically they could. Historically this was the case. Historically x y z happened,' and that's a comforting bridge that connects me to how I feel as a woman – and I'm a pretty independent, strong woman – some people say! [Laughs.] And pretty outspoken! So I dance with it.

ME: Clearly, you've taken Ifa's feminist message to heart.

AYELE: The world needs women to heal this planet. Otherwise it's going to self-destruct. And that means women have to be willing to take responsibility, to take our power back and to walk in it authentically and in harmony with nature. Embracing the female aspects is the only way we're going to bring harmony back to this world and to elevate it.

ME: Ayele, thanks so much.

Labor Day

THE SUN WAS fierce; the wind harsh. Sand stung my eyes as we walked among the dunes on Anastasia Island. One last ritual remained before I packed my bags and headed home.

A mile wide, this ruggedly attractive barrier island is where the Matanzas River meets the Northeast Atlantic coastline – and, for our purposes, that day, where Oshun meets Yemoja. A water goddess, too, Yemoja presides over fertility and the ocean.

Vassa was dressed, as usual, in her trademark white linen; I was in my swim suit, gagging for a swim. A female turtle crossed our path. Vassa claimed this to be an excellent omen – but not as far as I was concerned; ahead of us red flags were flapping about in the wind, putting paid to my last attempt at an ocean dip.

'Do you ever swim here?'

'Me? Never! Vassa replied. 'I've seen too many sharks washed up on this coastline, and the waves are so high.'

Coquina shells were a-plenty there, too – and razor shells. I put on my flipflops. Vassa expressed surprise at the number of

196

people picnicking on the beach.

'I brought you here as it's usually so peaceful; no-one around.'

'That's because it's Labor Day,' I told her.

'Ah. I hadn't realised.'

Since getting caught out by the hurricane I'd taken to watching the news every day. That morning I'd discovered that the first Monday of September is designated an annual public holiday in the United States, to commemorate the workforce that built the country. Families headed for the coast on Labor Day, much as they did in England on a sunny bank holiday. All well and good, but I felt queasy at the thought of having an audience when we performed the ritual.

Vassa led me to the ocean's edge, where she untied a bag containing twenty-four live shrimps. This ritual was, she informed me, a prelude to my very final shedding. We waded into the choppy brine together. I had a heart-sink moment when she instructed me to offer the shrimps to Yemoja, one by one, with a prayer for each and every one of them. It was aquatic *Groundhog Day* again. I really *had* run out of prayers now – the last one, I reckoned, had scuttled off on the back of a hermit crab. But as Vassa recited a passionate *orike* to the goddess, I put myself through the motions – more mindful of the rip tides and the sun burning my unprotected back than I was of placating this powerful water deity. If Yemoja had let me have my swim I might have been more enthusiastic.

We wandered along the shoreline in silence until we reached a wide estuary where the Matanzas meets the Atlantic. Vassa stood still and gazed out at the water.

'I've been meaning to tell you, I met up with Gene again.'

'You did? How is he?'

'It's looking good. We did another reading. This time it was without fear.'

What had come up for Gene in this one was that rather than escape to Colombia, he had another choice: to change everything. He'd since made the decision to stop doing anything illegal and was winding up his current business. Gene had also found a good lawyer, and the police were off his back. He'd told Vassa he had a percentage of Native American blood in him and was now applying for an *ayahuasca* licence through the Native American Foundation. It was looking likely that he'd be granted a special permit.

'He's becoming more involved with Ifa', Vassa smiled happily. 'He says he's never been as excited about his life as he is today… C'mon let's get in this water.'

A little way upstream the river was calmer. We waded in knee-deep. Once I'd thrown some coins into the water for Oshun, as instructed, Vassa asked me to lie on my back. The river there was shallow but pleasantly buoyant and cooling. She knelt down and cradled my head in her lap. Whispering Yoruba incantations, she leant over me and massaged my scalp. It didn't take long before I stopped wondering what Labor Day families were making of this Sapphic-looking scenario, and succumbed to a deeply relaxing dreaminess…

…I was back in the Sacred Groves. Waxbills circled the azure skies. The leaves of the baobab trees were rustling in the breeze. Rainbow fish danced around me as I bathed in Oshun's river, imbued with the goddess's tender presence. I wanted to stay forever in this timeless, euphoric zone…

'OK, we're done,' said Vassa, getting abruptly to her feet. I sat up, disoriented.

'I was so chilled…so peaceful,' she said, 'until I became aware that something – something very ancient – was making its way up and out through the top of your head.'

'What!?'

'Not sure – an entity of some sort…the colour of dark mustard…octopus-like tentacles.'

'Now I'm totally freaked out.'

'Don't be. Those tentacles came out willingly…they wanted out… And then…then they just floated away with the current…'

I was lost for words, unable to sensibly process what she'd just told me. All I knew was that I wanted to remove myself from this weirdness. Why was I oblivious to the departure of this horrid mustardy thing – or even to its existence in the first place? I may well have been floating around in La La Land, but surely I would have felt *something* when this psychic tumour slid out of my head?

'I'm going for a swim, Vassa.'

'Yeah, you do that. I need to clear myself.'

I swam downstream into the deeper part of the estuary – but Yemoja had other plans. Her powerful currents tugged me away from the safety of the river and into her dangerous ocean waters. I made my way back upstream, and, from a distance, observed Vassa. Still fully-clothed and waist-deep in water, with her head flung back and muttering incantations, she waved her arms about in a synchronous, tai chi-like fashion. I tried not to stare. What, I wondered, was going on in her head at that moment? I couldn't fathom this woman.

As I splashed about in the shallows, still unwilling to return to the shore, I found myself comparing Vassa and Adunni. Both women had been shrewd enough to recognise the labyrinthine depth of a culture that had too often been dismissed as primitive; brave enough to roll up their sleeves and mine this hidden African gold; canny enough to exploit the empowering energy the *orisha* offered. They were also highly intelligent women; psychologically aware, brave and creative, and both, at times, exuded an aura of mystery, but the similarity ended there. As a rule, Vassa emanated more of a motherly vibe and I'd grown to like her enormously, but she struck me as being essentially a healer who worked through the medium of *orisha*. Adunni, on the other hand, I would be forever in awe of. She was very much the high priestess; an aloof, sage-like, ancient soul; part *orisha* herself.

After twenty or so minutes Vassa came walking towards me with outstretched hands, her hair and clothes wet through and streaked with seaweed.

'Hey, feel these. They're like bunches of electric eels. It's the healing energy.'

I touched her hands and she was right. They were pulsing and trembling simultaneously, and very hot.

'What *was* that entity?' I asked. 'It's totally spooked me.'

'Relax. It was probably just a very, very ancient, rather dark ancestor. Let's get some ice cream.'

'Was it my ancestor witch you said you'd seen in that photograph you took of me at Ola Olu?'

'Maybe, maybe... You're gonna feel much lighter now it's bin shed.'

She went on to tell me about how she'd once healed a Vietnam vet of crippling survivor's guilt. After he'd connived to get out of a certain tour of duty, the plane he should have flown out on was shot down, killing all his GI buddies. He'd suffered years of self-recrimination: he believed he should be dead too. So Vassa decided to perform a ceremony which involved burying him alive at Ola Olu. Not quite how I would have handled this psychological trauma in my clinic, but the symbolic burial apparently did the trick and cured his survivor's guilt.

Vassa was on a high as we headed back to the car, making a positive connection or sharing a joke with everything and everyone we passed: a child eating a piece of melon; a dog with a thorn in its paw – she took out her tweezers; a gnarled old tree she wanted to stroke; a family struggling to light their BBQ.

'What helps you to stay so upbeat, Vassa?

'Doing The Work.'

'You mean the practice of Ifa?'

'Yes. And when negativity comes along, I kill it. She licked her ice cream. 'You should do the same. Just kill it.'

Back at her house, Vassa offered to do a reading for me using the divining *opele* given to her by Adunni. This was the last time I'd be seeing her, and she wanted me to have a good send-off. She gave the sixteen palm nuts in her hand a vigorous shake. What came up in this reading was all about me 'moving forward and doing The Work.'

'Get ready,' she gushed. 'You're gonna take off. There's a lot of work to do. Put your heart into it. Find sweetness in it.'

We traipsed into her office to offer some honey to a carving of Ogun to help me find 'sweetness'.

Ye Ye Ye O

I COULDN'T put it off any longer. Almost every day since being in Florida I'd cycled past another kind of sacred grove on my favourite riverside path. I was flying home that evening and I was determined, finally, to enter in.

Kiddies' wind chimes suspended from branches tinkled in the breeze. Nailed to the trunk of a red maple tree in this semi-circular glade-garden, close to the river, was the faded photograph of a chemotherapy-bald teenager in a hospital gown smiling into the camera, his arms around his mom and dad. Propped up beside a hand-carved child's seat, dedicated to *Our Little Angel*, was a Barbie doll wrapped in Clingfilm; attached to the tiny chair, a laminated photograph of a pale, blond young girl with a fairy wand clasped in both hands. Beneath a palm bower I almost stepped on a wreath of artificial violets draped over a slab of stone engraved with a dedication to a young man of twenty-four, which read: *Son, from you we learnt that what is most important in life is to love and be loved.*

The sheer intensity of love and loss that emanated from the butterfly-rich Children's Memorial Garden was tangible. Possibly the most pure, unselfish love we humans feel is that of a parent for their child. I cycled on until I found a bench at the river's edge, where I parked the bike and gazed numbly down at the water; my avoidance, until now, of the memorial garden had been about putting grief on hold.

Oshun is the *orisha* who was allocated the task of granting children. During the Oshun Festival in Oshogbo, women come from as far away as China seeking fertility cures. She's also the *orisha* who represents love. The original male primordials sent by Olodumare (God) to create the earth initially failed in their task because they'd kept Oshun/Love out of the equation. It wasn't until they included her that the world could come into being.

The gently flowing river calmed me. I took my copy of *Yoruba Myths* by Adunni's first husband, Ulli Beier, from my rucksack – and read, once again, his English translation of a traditional Yoruba *oriki* dedicated to Oshun.

> *Brass and parrot feathers on a velvet skin.*
> *White cowrie shells on black buttocks.*
> *Her eyes sparkle in the forest,*
> *like the sun on the river.*
> *She is the wisdom of the forest.*
> *She is the wisdom of the river.*
> *Where doctors failed, she cures with fresh water.*
> *Where medicine is impotent, she cures with cool water.*
> *She cures the child and does not charge the father.*
> *She feeds the barren woman with honey,*
> *and her dry body swells up like a juicy palm fruit.*
> *Oh how sweet is the touch of a child's hand.*

I was struck, yet again, by the beauty, compassion and contemporaneousness of this ancient *orike* in which Oshun is depicted as both sensual and nurturing; a truly rounded vision of womanhood. I felt blessed to have encountered this wholesome goddess. For the first time I recited an incantation to summon her: 'Yeye, Ye Ye O' (Chief Mother) I whispered over and over again. 'Yeye, Ye Ye O… Yeye, Ye Ye O…'

The incantation had a hypnotic effect; I lost track of time… Sunlight sparkled on rivulets of undulating water… I felt myself merging with the river…with Oshun. I closed my eyes and recalled my most precious memory of Adunni…

Sally was in the front passenger seat having a scratchy conversation with her driver. We'd delayed our return to Lagos by a day to give Adunni a lift to the Groves, as her transport had let her down. Sally's driver wasn't at all happy about this, insisting that the car was due to go into the garage that day for more repairs. I was taking advantage of the lift to squeeze a few more nuggets of wisdom out of the high priestess, and she was being quite obliging. I sensed she had truly warmed towards me – at last. The day before, when I was on my way to the Groves to take some last-minute photographs, she'd insisted on lending me her tatty black umbrella as protection from the sun. I felt genuinely honoured.

'Are you working on the shrines today, Adunni, or will you be performing rituals?'

'Rituals.'

'What form will they take?'

'This isn't something I can say much about. It is *eewo*.'

'*Eewo*?'

'Taboo.'

'I understand.'

'Do you?' She looked at me closely. 'Do you *really* understand why my rituals are *eewo*?'

I withered. 'No…no, not really.'

'Why do you think we do not know the details of our past lives and those to come?'

'Could be traumatic, I suppose.'

'It would give rise to such bewilderment and identity confusion. For reasons of human protection this knowledge is taboo. The power of a reality-shifting experience – especially of a deific nature – diminishes once it is spoken about.'

'Words are inadequate, I suppose.'

'Words reduce the awe of the experience. Just as those who have returned to life after a clinical death struggle to describe their experience, so, too, do the *orisha* defy semantics.'

In the front seat the discussion was becoming heated. Sally was demanding to know why her relatively new car kept breaking down and having to go into the garage for repairs almost every week. The driver snorted and shrugged his shoulders. Not long after this trip to Oshogbo, Sally would discover that over several months her sneaky driver had been surreptitiously selling off the car's good engine parts and replacing them with rubbish ones.

We pulled up at the entrance to the Sacred Groves. I helped Adunni climb out of the car. We were keen to drive back to Lagos before it grew dark, but she seemed hesitant, once we'd dropped her off, to enter the Groves.

'Do you have water?' she asked, dropping her bag and leaning against the car, coughing. I motioned to the driver to switch the engine off. Sally fetched a flask from the boot and poured some water into a plastic cup.

'Thank you.' Adunni sipped the water in silence, then she

handed back the cup and looked closely at us both. 'You know, you have your gods and goddesses too.'

Registering our puzzled expressions, she continued, 'Buddhism has many parallels with Ifa... What is essential is that no one religion or culture thinks itself superior to others. What we must all have in common is respect for life and the environment.'

'You've certainly demonstrated that,' said Sally, spreading a cotton wrapper onto the dried grass. 'Why don't you sit down, Adunni, you look exhausted.'

She shook her head. 'The heat, it will pass... We may think that cultures on this planet exist independently of each other, but they do not. We are all essential pieces in the vast jigsaw of humankind.'

For some reason I giggled – nervousness, perhaps, at the portentousness of these statements.

'All my life,' she said, giving me a stern look, 'I have believed in the psychic unity of humankind... But some sections of humanity are trying their hardest to blow each other up, yes, and Mother Earth, too...It is of extreme importance that we all try our hardest to make enormous efforts in the opposite direction – to right the balance.' She motioned towards the forest. 'This is, in part, why I have struggled, for so many years, to preserve these Sacred Groves.'

Adunni gave us each a piercing look. 'You understand that, girls, don't you?'

Impatient to leave, the driver started the engine up. She glanced at her watch. Grasping each of us by the wrist she graced us with a rare, beatific smile.

'You two are angels,' she said. Then she picked up her bag, and without looking back at our astonished faces, strolled off into the Sacred Groves.

Unbeknown to me then, this would be my very last glimpse of Adunni.

A breeze started up. In the distance I could hear the tinkling of the wind chimes in the memorial garden. The sun began to set; I pedalled slowly back to the marina and returned my bike to the shop I'd hired it from.

Afterword

As FASCINATED as I am by Ifa, I feel unable to commit to it. While I agree with the late Berkeley professor, William Bascom, who was the western world's foremost authority on the religion, that Ifa is powerful and it works (Sally met and fell in love with a wonderful man the month after returning from Florida), in the final analysis I want my joys and sorrows to be my own responsibility – not the whim of an external deity whom I have to pamper or placate with offerings and sacrifices.

But as a Buddhist I love how Ifa respects the dignity of all living beings and the natural world. And as a psychotherapist, I take my hat off to this ancient belief system which has mapped out the human psyche so ingeniously. Ifa is a complex, life-affirming belief system, which offers a strong, clear example of Africa's cultural depth, acuity and potential. Perhaps the time has come for it to travel beyond Africa and the Yoruba diaspora; to share a few of its precious secrets with the rest of the world.

On the face of it, I'd made the trip to Florida, to Ola Olu, to fulfil my promise to Adunni to participate in Oshun rituals. Once I'd returned home, however, I couldn't escape the feeling that, subconsciously, it was Adunni I'd gone in search of; it was she who I'd longed to connect with once more; Adunni the woman – not the high priestess. We all need mentors. Although she herself was never aware of it, Adunni has occupied the role of mentor in my life for many, many years. I'm also mindful of the fact that if it hadn't been for Daisaku Ikeda, my Buddhist mentor, having the energy and compassion to spread the Buddhism I practise, globally, I'd never have met Dr Afolabi, whose suggestion it was I should *check out* this *high priestess of the goddess Oshun* all those years ago.

Why do I consider Adunni a mentor? Apart from being a brilliant artist, she had the bravery to embrace and champion a culture profoundly different from her own, and, during an era of apartheid, when mixed-race liaisons were frowned upon, she turned her back on convention and married Ayansola Alarape, a black drummer. She nurtured young artists and had the vision and the energy to set up her globally successful School of New Sacred Art. She stood up to Christians, Muslims and property developers intent on destroying the Sacred Groves, and risked her life sitting in front of the bulldozers they'd sent to raze her beloved shrines. Even in her eighties, she climbed ladders and scaffolding to work on her magnificent sculptural sanctuaries for the gods, and battled for years to have the Groves declared a World Heritage Site. She has proved herself to be a great advertisement for her goddess.

Adunni broke so many rules. She didn't suffer fools gladly, but she was truly authentic – and, yes, that made her appear eccentric to many – but what the hell? This was a woman whose humanity was so deep she was prepared to risk her life harbouring Jews and working with the Resistance. If I could be half as brave as she was I'd die happy.

As for Oshun, in an exciting development that no one, myself least of all, could have predicted, the goddess has now gone global. At the 2017 Grammys, pregnant with twins (so cherished by the Yoruba), the American singer, Beyoncé, came on stage, channelling the goddess. Few performers possess the dignity, self-assurance and verve to appear as the iconic goddess of womanhood. Looking magnificent in a golden bikini, sequined gown and sun-ray crown, the singer considered the most successful black female artist on the planet, was bowed to by a sea of black, female dancers as they fluttered about the stage.

Beyoncé's celebrated performance was enthusiastically reported by media and social media the world over – with the exception of certain Christian Fundamentalist outlets who accused the singer of being a devil worshipper.

Around the world, Africa-savvy academics were wheeled out to give interviews about this mysterious goddess of beauty, prosperity and love, and Ifa, the little-known belief-system that spawned her.

'Beyoncé is speaking to the world, she is speaking to America,' claimed Dr Jacob Olupona, Professor of African Religious Traditions and Chair of the Committee on African Studies at the Harvard Divinity School. 'She is educating the masses on Oshun. She is seeing how indigenous spirituality can be a powerful tool for changing the world.'

The Grammys were not the first occasion on which Beyoncé made an appearance as Oshun. Her album, *Lemonade*, is packed with references to Ifa and the diaspora. The music video for 'Hold Up', the second single on the album, features the singer completely submerged in a room filled with water, writhing around and levitating, before emerging, triumphant, through ornamental doors and Grecian columns, in a flowing, golden gown, to descend a long flight of steps – a massive torrent of water following in her wake. In a song that is believed by many to be about her anger with her husband Jay Z for his alleged infidelity, she proceeds, with Oshun-like, righteous anger at her betrayal, to roam through an urban neighbourhood, with a smile on her face, smashing fire hydrants with a baseball bat, releasing her rage in torrents of water.

Her reverberations were felt in Great Britain, too. Thanks to Beyoncé, the goddess actually managed to make it into the *Daily Mail*. The paper even included a picture of her shrine in the Sacred Groves, built by Adunni. Perhaps Oshun's time has come.

Glossary

Adunni Orisha – honorary title meaning beloved of the gods
Agbada – a long, wide-sleeve robe worn by West African men
Aje – psychic power
Alafia – blessings and peace; a greeting
Alhaji – an honorific title in West Africa for someone who has visited Mecca
Arelagbayi – carvers of sacred images of the *orisha*
Ashe – power, spirit. 'Amen' in Ifa
Babalawo – high priest of Ifa
Candomblé – the Brazilian version of Ifa
Ebo – a sacrifice or offering
Eshu – a male *orisha* invoked before a ritual; messenger of the gods
Fila – traditional Nigerian hat worn by men
Ibeji – carved, consecrated doll given to a mother when a twin dies
Ifa – the ancient belief system of the Yoruba peoples

Igbeyawo – the Yoruba word for marriage

Ilé-Ifè– the birthplace of Ifa; the oldest city of the Yoruba people

Iyami – primordial female energies which protect women

Iyanifa – Mother of Divination/high priestess of Ifa

Lae Lae – Yoruba concept of non-linear, eternal time

Lucumí – a version of Ifa practised in Cuba

Mami Wata (Mammy Water) – a name for water goddesses including Oshun

Nana Buuken – the most ancient of the primordial female energies

Oba – ruler or king

Obatala – a male orisha of healing and wisdom

Odu – the oracles of the Yoruba system of knowledge and divination

Odu Ose Otura – an oracle concerning gender equality

Ogun – a male *orisha* of iron; a warrior

Oku – a male *orisha* of the soil

Olodumare – the Yoruba name for the divine creator; God

Ori – the head; an individual's divinity; spiritual destiny

Oluwo – Master of Secrets: the highest level a high priest can attain

Omilade – a nurturing, mermaid-like female *orisha*

Onile – a female *orisha* connected to the earth

Opele – a divination chain usually made of cowrie shells

Oriki – verses which praise the *orisha*

Orisha – the Ifa pantheon of gods and goddesses

Oshogbo – Nigerian town purported to be the birthplace of Oshun

Orumila – a male *orisha* of knowledge

Oshun – a female *orisha* of love, beauty, creativity; a river in Oshogbo

Oya – a female *orisha* of wind and transformation

Santería – a version of Ifa practised in Cuba and the Caribbean

Shango – a male *orisha* of war

Yemoja – a female *orisha* of the ocean and fertility

Yoruba – an ethnic group residing in West Africa and in countries affected by the Yoruba Diaspora which resulted from the slave trade

Acknowledgements

Since my first meeting with her in 1986 I've longed to share Suzanne Wenger's story with a wider audience. With the publication of this book I'm delighted that I'm finally able to do so. I'm grateful to my dear friend Dr Bamgboye Afolabi for introducing me to such an inspiring female mentor, and to Daisaku Ikeda, my mentor in Buddhism, for his hope-fuelled vision of Africa, and his admonition to never give up.

I'm beholden to my sister, Sally Crombie, who not only accompanied me on parts of this journey but who has also, along with her fellow artist, Sophie Pasiewicz, produced a strikingly beautiful book cover.

Iyanifa Vassa and Oluwo Phil, the founders of the Ifa Foundation, generously shared their knowledge of Ifa and oversaw the rituals I undertook in Florida, as well as being warm, wise and hospitable hosts. I would also like to thank Iyanifa Ayele Kumari in Missouri for allowing me to interview her for this book.

I'm most appreciative of the work my agent, Jennifer Barclay, has undertaken on my behalf and for her unceasingly invaluable advice. I would also like to thank Clio Mitchell for her constructive suggestions and her expertise in editing the book, and my publisher, Dan Hiscocks, for his enthusiasm, encouragement and willingness to take risks. My thanks also go to the Eye/Lightning Books team for their commitment and professionalism, and to Sue Amaradivakara for her PR initiatives..

Sue and Neil, my sister and brother, have generously provided helpful feedback. And, as always, my husband David has proved a patient reader and a wonderfully supportive presence.

Last but not least, I'm indebted to the enchanting deity whose existence has made possible the writing of this book: the goddess Oshun.

About the author

DIANE Esguerra is a writer, a psychotherapist and a traveller. The author of *Junkie Buddha: A Journey of Discovery in Peru*, Diane is also the recipient of a Geneva-Europe Television Award and a *Time Out* Theatre Award. She lives in Surrey with her husband David.

By the same author

Junkie Buddha

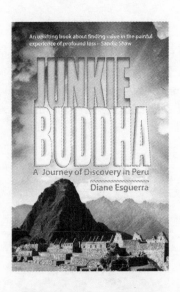

Published in 2015 by Eye Books
ISBN: 9781903070994

£8.99

OUR HEALING journeys differ. Some move country or hit the bottle. Diane's healing journey was travel. Her son loved travelling and mountain climbing in South America. He'd walked the Inca Trail and longed to return to the sacred citadel of Machu Picchu. On the first anniversary of his death, fragile and aching with grief, she travelled alone to Peru to scatter his ashes there. Diane's adventures en route were by turns scary, electrifying and humorous: flying over the Nazca Lines; a consultation with an Inca witch; an accidental brush with Peruvian porn. She immersed herself in the culture, and Peru reconnected her with life. This is a story about profound loss leading to spiritual gain. And it's a story about love.

Read on for reviews of *Junkie Buddha* on pp220-221.

Read a sneak preview of the first two chapters of *Junkie Buddha* on pp222-242.

IN PRAISE OF *JUNKIE BUDDHA*

This is an inspiring and uplifting book about finding innate value in the most intense and painful experience of profound loss.

Sandie Shaw, singer

I could not put this gripping travel memoir down. What a refreshing change from the endless stream of ghost-written celebrity outpourings! *Junkie Buddha* is moving and enlightening. It deserves the widest possible readership.

Julia Stephenson, author, journalist

A heart-wrenching and uplifting story of one woman's tragedy, transformation and, ultimately, triumph, made all the more powerful because every word is true – and because Diane Esguerra is a very fine writer.

Eddy Canfor-Dumas, novelist, award-winning screenwriter

If the purpose of personal narratives is to make sense out of one's life then Diane Esguerra's excellent memoir will, I suspect, present not only an invaluable insight into how telling your story may save you from it, but also achieve redemptive potential for all those who have suffered a similar bereavement. Above all *Junkie Buddha: A Journey of Discovery in Peru* demonstrates how the healing process is to pass from the narration of trauma as hurt feelings into the narration of trauma as an experience of deep significance.

Marina Cantacuzino, founder of The Forgiveness Project

Highly recommended…a must-read to synthesise your being.

Ali Zaidi

Diane's book takes you on both a geographical and spiritual journey to a place of healing and ultimately to a place of peace in mind and heart. For anyone going through the grief journey of losing a loved one to addiction I highly recommend this mother's story as an opportunity to reflect on your own experiences and hopefully find a way out of the maze of emotions Diane takes us through. Ultimately, you will feel uplifted and strengthened by sharing this journey with her.

Elizabeth Burton-Phillips, author of *Mum, Can You Lend Me Twenty Quid?: What drugs did to my family*, **founder & CEO, DrugFAM**

Diane's extraordinary journey of a lifetime is a brilliant and poetic evocation of deep loss, set in dramatic and fascinating landscapes. Unforgettable.

Sue Parrish, director, Sphinx Theatre Company

It's not very often a book reduces me to tears, but Junkie Buddha is the kind of read that reaches deep into your soul while also pulling firmly on the heart strings.

Shelley Wilson, blogger

Diane Esguerra's eloquent writing and self-deprecating humour make this a surprisingly rewarding and uplifting reads. The journey is a courageous one; so, too, is her willingness to share raw emotion with her reader and her determination to create both meaning and value out of some truly heart-breaking life experiences.

Therapy Today

Chapter One

Lost Treasures of the World

WHY ME?

I never thought it would happen to me. It happened to other mothers – yes, and fathers too. I'd seen them on the evening news, puffy-eyed, bewildered, blinking away tears. The camera zooms in to the photograph of the son as they like to remember him, in his school blazer (eyes still shining then) grinning toothlessly at the school photographer. Or the daughter as a teenager, astride a mountain bike in the Pyrenees, tanned and ponytailed.

I never thought it would happen to me. But in 2005 it did. I discovered my child Sacha, a man now, a man who had never practised yoga, slumped over in child-pose on a beer-stained rug; his alabaster back cold to my touch; a half-empty syringe at his side; daytime television drowned out by the weeping of his dogs and the howling of police sirens.

My future ambushed.

These mothers on the television – clutching handkerchiefs or their husbands' hands – I used to think they put themselves through this ordeal in order to draw the public's attention to a pressing social issue, start a campaign, establish a foundation to honour his or her memory. But then I understood they did it to avoid waking up in the morning with the feeling that the very heart of their lives has been surgically extracted without anaesthetic. Although they yearn to escape to the realm the beloved has made an untimely entry into – without their permission – they're too considerate to inflict this same agony on their living loved ones. So what do they do instead? They search for meaning; for a purpose to rein themselves back from the lurking abyss.

In the weeks that followed Sacha's death I duly busied myself applying to a charitable trust for funding to set up a project that would in some way honour my son. I wanted to do something to help teenagers who had been abused in childhood and who would, more than likely, go on to self-harm, harm others or abuse substances. But my burnt-out heart wasn't really in it. I needed a break from that all-too-familiar world, and it was a relief when the funding didn't come through.

But the void continued to terrorise me. As a Buddhist I believed in the preciousness of life and the concept of 'turning poison into medicine' – that suffering – however deep – could, ultimately, prove beneficial. But what value could possibly be created from this?

My daily mantra had become 'Why me?' 'Why me?'

'I'm not a junkie, Mum,' Sacha used to say. 'I'm someone with a habit.'

And I'd convinced myself I could help him break that habit. Defeat wasn't an option I'd allowed myself to consider; too much was at stake.

My son wasn't the archetypal junkie you see in the movies with hollowed-out, shifty eyes, greasy hair, and thieving, nicotine-stained fingers. Yes, he smoked roll-ups, but that was as far as it went. He was curious about many things in life and had a lively enquiring mind. More than he loved heroin, Sacha loved ancient Hispanic history, and climbing mountains.

For Christmas, the week before his death, he'd given me a large, glossy, illustrated book called *Lost Treasures of the World*. I read how Conquistador Francisco Pizarro captured the Inca emperor Atahualpa in Peru and promised him his freedom if his people were able to fill a 'ransom room' full of gold. For months the Incas laboured day and night to bring gold and treasure from all over their empire. But once the ransom room was full, Pizarro killed him anyway.

How I empathised with those Incas who, like me, had done everything, everything in their power, to save Atahualpa. How cheated they must have felt after his death.

How cheated I felt.

It was, he said, the best Christmas he'd had for years. We had tears in our eyes as Sacha played the blues again on his harmonica. Finally on a decent drugs programme, I thought he'd turned a corner at last. Then, after some crazy partying on New Year's Eve, one last fling resulted, according to the coroner, in 'accidental death from a heroin overdose'.

And I lost my treasure.

Peru stayed with me, though. Sacha's ashes sat in a wooden urn – not on the mantelpiece but, out of respect for his shyness, tucked away in a corner of the living room under the voluminous palm tree he'd bought me many Mother's Days ago. The ashes wanted to be scattered – but where? I already knew. I'd known all along.

For the last few years of his life, all Sacha had wanted was to go back to South America. Brought up in England but half Colombian, he'd travelled the continent extensively, and had hiked the Inca Trail before it became a popular gap-year thing. He often recalled the moment when, dead on his feet with hunger and exhaustion, he reached the end of the trail and felt his spirit soar as he watched the sun rise over the Inca citadel of Machu Picchu.

'One of the coolest moments of my life, Mum. When I'm better I want to see that sunrise again, and I want to take you with me.'

I had the feeling he still did.

But the perilous, futile trail of recovery we'd been limping along together for years had left me depleted and confused. I'd morphed into an auto-pilot-crisis-management zombie with no time to process where and why it had all gone wrong, or the head-space to write about it. Some form of reflective, healing journey might be the answer.

But was Peru, with its conquistadors, Shining Path Maoist guerrillas and heartbreaking poverty, a sensible choice? It had never been on my tourist radar. The country was, however, home to that most sacred – and much-visited – site in Latin America, the site that Sacha most loved. So it would, quite simply, have to be.

Already, it was almost a year since he'd died, but was I brave enough yet to make the journey to Machu Picchu to scatter my son's ashes? I'd spent the last few years fending off my terror of death; now I was afraid of life. The tectonic plates of my world had imploded. I was in fragments. There was a permanent knot in my stomach – the severed umbilical cord.

All I knew was that I had to go soon. And that I had to go alone.

The funeral parlour was conveniently situated at the end of my road. Lee, the bulbous, balding undertaker who ran this 100-year-old family business, was expecting me. In our dealings to date he'd shown a concern above and beyond the call of duty. Today there was a silent understanding between us: we both knew that, for me, what was about to take place would be deeply disturbing. Lee showed me into his office and pulled out a chair. I handed over the wooden urn and he left the room.

My flight to Peru went via the United States. On Lee's advice I'd contacted the American Embassy in London who informed me that because airport security might wish to examine the ashes, they had to be removed from the sealed urn and transported in an unsealed bag.

Five minutes later, Lee returned, watery-eyed, and apologetically presented me with a nondescript plastic bag containing all that remained of my beautiful son. Had that powerful, vibrant energy that once constituted Sacha really metamorphosed into nothing more than a bag of gritty, grey dust? Even if I were a seasoned agnostic I'd find that hard to believe. Surely, such energy could never die?

Starlings circled overhead as I stumbled back up the road to my house, clutching the plastic bag to my chest, tears splattering the pavement. The postman, who had delivered our mail for years, propped his bike up against the wall and stared at me curiously. If he only knew that inside the plastic bag were the remains of that friendly young guy who kept a firm hold on those lively German Shepherds of his when he answered the door – drum 'n' bass blaring out from behind.

Once home, I knelt down on the living room floor. Steeling myself, I transferred the ashes into a hand-embroidered orange silk pouch and placed them inside the small, expensive, black leather rucksack I'd purchased for their transportation.

David, my partner of 10 years, was in tears when he dropped me off at the airport.

'You don't have to get on that plane, you know. There's still time.'

He was worried I wouldn't be strong enough to see it through – or worse, that I might not come back.

He looked exhausted. David worked in television news, and had been up all night editing. The last few years had been almost as testing for him as they had for me. Our marriage had been tested too, but it was the third for both of us and from its outset we were determined to make it work. Our Buddhist chanting helped. I was grateful to David for never putting me in the position where I had to choose between him and Sacha.

'Promise you won't go mental on that motorbike,' I said, trying to deflect the threat of danger from myself. He nodded unconvincingly. Conscious that grief had made me more selfish, I hugged my husband goodbye and walked away.

On the flight from Gatwick to Atlanta the stewardess insisted that my precious cargo be placed in the overhead locker. I tried to distract myself by wondering, as we flew over the wilderness of the Arctic, whether Sacha, too, could see the glaciers, the fjords and the intricate patterns of light dancing above Greenland's ice sheet. He'd had such a love of nature and, for that matter, of life. Strange, really, as at birth he'd not wanted to make an appearance and had to be induced. A few weeks after he finally slid out, calmly and contentedly sucking his thumb, the health visitor made me take him to the doctor for a check-up because he almost never cried. I guess he was saving it up for later.

'Well, Maaaam?' the American immigration official growled. 'Why are you travelling on your own to Peru?'

His glare remained fixed. Dare I risk telling him the truth? No. I lied and said that my husband would be joining me at Christmas.

'That all your luggage?' he asked, pointing at the rucksack. 'I checked in a suitcase at Gatwick.'

He leafed through my passport.

'Employed?'

Again, I hesitated. 'Writer' might sound too nebulous and only confirm his suspicion that I could, indeed, be a drugs mule heading for the coca fields of the Andes. I opted for 'psychotherapist' instead. He grunted and let me through. It can be useful, sometimes, having two professions.

For the world's busiest airport, Atlanta's cavernous concourse was surprisingly devoid of passengers. As if to compensate, a regiment of television screens blasted out CNN in all directions: a trauma expert was explaining that the victims of Hurricane Katrina were still reeling from shock and would need counselling for years. News footage from the summer showing desperate New Orleanians bobbing up and down in the water clutching their pets, or clinging to the sides of rescue boats, uncomfortably mirrored my own inner landscape.

On the television screen above the red Formica bar, Condoleezza Rice was busy trying to convince the world that the CIA weren't engaging in torture off US soil. I ordered a large, expensive glass of Pinot Grigio.

Condoleezza was replaced, a few sound-bites later, by John Lennon and the announcement that today was the 25th anniversary of his death. Archive footage of John and Yoko came on, accompanied, predictably, by the song Imagine. I felt a pang of envy for Yoko. She got to share her grief with millions of empathic others, and collective global grieving had helped to keep John's memory alive. But perhaps she would have preferred her grief to be private and hidden away in a body-bag like mine.

'I'm sorry, but he has to remain in the bag in the chapel of rest,' Lee had gently explained, handing me a box of tissues. 'Your boy was a user. It's Health and Safety who won't permit it, love, not me.'

I sipped my wine and imagined 'my boy' was perched on the bar stool beside me, complaining, as usual, about American beer and George Bush. I'm asking him whether Peruvian beer is any better. He raises his glass. '*Sí Señora, muchísimo!*' He chuckles, and starts to brag about all the really cool pre-Columbian sites he's going to take me to.

A tannoy announcing the departure of my flight to Lima catapulted me back into reality. 'Get a grip!' I ordered myself as I gulped back the wine and headed for my gate. At the security barrier I was instructed to remove my shoes and join a short queue. I placed the rucksack in a tray and watched as a wheelchair-bound octogenarian lady was ordered to vacate her wheelchair, remove her beige sling-backs and hobble through the security door. She was hardly your typical shoe-bomber. Would they want to examine the ashes – or worse still confiscate them?

I began fighting my own war against terror: the thought of a stranger sifting through the delicate remains of my beloved son made my stomach heave. Fortunately for me, the old lady's distress distracted the guard monitoring the security screen. He barely glanced at the interior of my rucksack and the ashes made it through.

As the Lima-bound plane took off into the funky gloom of Georgia the atmosphere started to feel lighter. Spanish was being spoken all around me. Keen to refresh mine, I eavesdropped on conversations, but struggled to keep up. The seat next to me was empty. That's Sacha's seat, I thought to myself. I closed my eyes and pictured him sitting beside me, his warm arm, with its neat Celtic tattoo and tarnished silver bracelets, nestling against mine.

As we approached the Southern Hemisphere a slender magnolia moon appeared above the wing of the plane, and beyond it, a smattering of stars lit up the indigo sky. I remembered Sacha telling me that the Incas believed each star was the protector of a particular species of animal or bird, and that, for these mysterious people, the dark shapeless voids which existed between the constellations held more symbolic meaning than the constellations themselves. I pressed my face to the window and examined the night sky. Would I ever be able to find meaning in the dark, shapeless void which had engulfed my own life? I wanted to get closer to my son on this trip, closer to his world.

We landed in Lima around midnight. As the queue inched its way towards immigration I chatted with a woman from Alabama who was on my flight. She'd been working for the IRS (US tax department) for over 15 years, she told me. Dressed from head to toe in denim with a badge-strewn straw hat pulled tightly over her chilli-red hair, she was, she said, intending to spend the night in the airport before taking an early morning flight to Iquitos. There she would meet up with a group of fellow ayahuasca travellers and continue for several more hours by bus and boat deep into the Amazon jungle for a week-long inner journey.

Ayahuasca was, she explained, a concoction made from hallucinogenic Amazonian plants that she'd be ingesting at a shamanic retreat. She hoped it would purge her of a toxic relationship she'd recently escaped from and revamp her stagnant life.

While admiring her courage, I couldn't help wondering

whether quitting her job and exploring Peru itself might be a better way of achieving the life change she was seeking than this week-long quick fix with, perhaps, a dose of dengue fever thrown in. But I kept my mouth shut. Deep down, I was hoping that Peru would fix me.

Reunited with my suitcase, I found myself in yet another buttock-clenching airport queue. A coiffeured customs official was presiding over a barrier above which there were two lights. I watched as she scrutinised each passenger then paused for several moments, like a sadistic game-show hostess, before pressing the button to illuminate either the red or the green light. On the other side of the barrier I could see the unfortunate 'reds' were having their luggage torn apart by guys in military uniform.

It was my turn. Fear rampaged inside me as I looked her in the eye. She stared back and pressed the green light. Dizzy with relief, I lurched through the barrier. The taxi driver, sent courtesy of my pre-booked hotel, ran over and grabbed my suitcase.

As we sped along El Paseo de la Republica in the early hours of the morning both Lima and my skinny young driver seemed as wide awake and adrenaline-fuelled as I was. Pizarro had daringly constructed his sprawling Ciudad de los Reyes – City of the Kings – on a quake-prone desert. I wound down the window and breathed in the sultry night air; I could smell the Pacific Ocean. Already I sensed that Peru would prove to be a land rich in culture and mystery.

The lively driver chattered incessantly, doubling back on himself to point out tastefully illuminated palaces, basilicas, fountains and haute-cuisine Limean eateries. I admired the mixture of stately colonial and ultra-modern architecture that he pointed out in this impromptu whirlwind tour, but turned down his offer to drive me around the barriadas (slum districts) which, he informed me, had been euphemistically re-named

Pueblos Jóvenes (Young Towns).

He eventually dropped me off outside my hotel, El Balcón Dorado, collected his fare from the weary-looking proprietor and accelerated off into the night. I suspected that his frenetic driving and effervescent commentary may have been fuelled by a touch of the indigenous joy powder.

The Golden Balcony was one of those scruffy hotels that had looked great on the internet, but I was too tired to care. A sleepy-eyed lady holding a wide-awake toddler welcomed me. She introduced herself as Martha, the proprietor's wife, and handed me a drink which resembled a Margarita. It was, she explained, a Pisco Sour – a white grape brandy from the port of Pisco, mixed with lime juice, egg white and Angostura bitters. It tasted divine.

My room, I was surprised to discover, came with a reasonably-sized ante-room stuffed with Euro-posh repro furniture, including a fake Napoleonic chaise-longue and a pair of Swiss mountain prints, framed ornately in gold plastic. I couldn't help but smile. At the very least I'd expected a print of the high Andes or an adobe Inca ruin or two. But never knowing quite where you might sleep or what you might be sleeping on, was, for me, an intriguing – and challenging – aspect of travel.

The room itself was pretty basic. A narrow partition led to a miniscule en-suite, comprising a rusty hand shower, a tiny basin and a creaky old loo. Compared to some of the mosquito-ridden bucket bath lodges in Africa that I'd stayed in over the years, this was luxury. And situated on the corner of Lima's Plaza Mayor, the historic heart of the city, El Balcón Dorado was about as central as I could get. After a tepid shower I flopped onto a lumpy old mattress and fell into a deep, dreamless sleep.

Chapter Two

Señor Ruiz: Finding the Courage

OVER BREAKFAST the next morning I dipped into my Peru guide, but flicking through its pages, the weariness of indecision descended upon me. Until two days earlier, this trip was going to be simple, so very simple. In November, I'd booked my month-long, non-refundable ticket, flying out to Lima in early December. I'd intended to go directly from there to Cusco, the launch pad for Machu Picchu. Once I'd scattered Sacha's ashes, my plan was to collapse in some tranquil, grief-friendly resort near the sea for the remainder of my stay, and chill. Then Roberto called.

To my surprise, he told me he wanted to attend the scattering – but insisted he couldn't make it to Peru until the end of December. His trip, he pointed out, would coincide with the first anniversary of Sacha's death on 2nd January. Roberto was my ex-husband – and the last person in the world I felt like meeting up with. But he was also Sacha's father, and I couldn't deny him the right to be present.

I hadn't seen Roberto since the funeral – nor had I wanted to. The partner in a Franco-Colombian architectural practice, Roberto, although he loved his son, had deliberately chosen to run its Africa office from Lagos – I suspected, to maintain a convenient distance between himself and Sacha's troubles. I was still angry with him for that.

In my heart, however, I knew the timing made sense. Perhaps Sacha himself wanted his ashes to be scattered on the first anniversary of his death by his mother and his father.

The prospect of being holed up in a hotel for nearly a month waiting for Roberto to arrive was grim, but did I have the courage to hit the road – with the ashes in tow – and explore Peru alone? Although I considered myself a seasoned traveller, the drain of the last few years, plus Sacha's death, had left me nervous and unsure of myself. In a complete quandary, I ventured out to change some traveller's cheques.

Ten minutes after leaving El Balcón Dorado, I was lost. The street names bore no resemblance to my map and Friday's bank queues were snaking around the plazas. I was thirsty, but without sol – the local currency – I couldn't even buy a bottle of water, let alone grab a taxi back to the sanctuary of the hotel. With its loud Latin jazz, traffic horns and growling street dogs, daytime Lima was certainly as lively and chaotic as I'd anticipated, and scary too: my guide book warned of 'strangle muggers' who roamed the streets, throttling and robbing unsuspecting tourists.

A robust young policeman strode over and asked me if I was lost. He offered to escort me to the Plaza Mayor where, he claimed, the banks weren't so busy. I didn't like to tell him that the Plaza Mayor was where I'd just come from. When I'd last visited South America I was constantly quizzed about the

Queen, but this young man showered me with questions about that new British royal: Wayne Rooney.

To keep him at my side for as long as possible, I dredged up all the superlative adjectives about Wayne and the Premier League my wobbly Spanish could muster, until we arrived at the end of his patch – and back at El Balcón Dorado.

An hour later I plucked up the courage to venture out again. Wandering down a narrow pedestrian side street I stopped to admire a Spanish-colonial building of glistening white marble. Amazingly, it was a bank; a cool, empty, queue-less bank and with a good exchange rate. Sunlight streamed in through the glass-domed ceiling. I felt a quick pang of excitement as the friendly cashier counted out my sol: I'd actually made it to Peru.

The cashier volunteered advice on what to see in Lima. Sightseeing was a great idea: it meant I could delay having to make a decision about what to do next.

The yellow stucco facade of the baroque Monastery of San Francisco was almost obscured by the sea of pigeons that swarmed around it – courtesy of the vendors selling bags of seed at its gates. To avoid the grungy flock I headed straight down a flight of steps and into the crypt.

This was a big mistake: skulls and femurs, meticulously arranged into neat concentric circles, mimicking the worst excesses of Pol Pot, gazed back at me. Over the last few centuries, these bone-filled, candlelit catacombs had witnessed some 70,000 burials. Someone coughed. I gasped. They jumped. A woman emerged from the shadows. We both laughed, relieved not to be alone in this subterranean cemetery. The woman, who was Dutch, told me it was her last day in Peru; I replied that it was my first. She said she envied me. I smiled and made my escape.

Blinking away sunlight, I hurried through a terracotta passageway lined with red geraniums into a cool, verdant courtyard surrounded by white, arched cloisters. My eyes alighted on a fading wall mural that depicted a 16th-century monk in the act of licking the leg of a leper. Perhaps this daft gesture of humility explained some of those dry old bones down below.

Heavy with tapestries, San Francisco Monastery also housed a library of antique texts dating back to the conquistadors, and its mainly Peruvian art collection included a Rubens and a Van Dyck. I stared, transfixed, at an 18th-century painting of the Pietà. Jesus! How that iconic image resonated. My mind flitted back to a summer in Rome three years earlier. I was in St Peter's, staring at Michelangelo's *Pietà*. Mary cradling the body of her dead son. My worst fear crystallised in stone. It was still only a fear then.

My eyes welled up yet again. Over the preceding year, man-size Kleenex and waterproof mascara had become my constant companions. The thick, curly, luxuriant hair, pale skin and large, soulful, grey-green eyes of the Christ in this painting bore a striking resemblance to my handsome son. Sacha was no Jesus, and I'd been a Buddhist for over 20 years, but I couldn't help thinking that Mary and I had quite a bit in common.

As I walked out of San Francisco's gates, a couple of shoeless street boys ran over. The elder of the two was wearing a torn, faded Manchester United shirt several sizes too big for him. They wanted to sell me a dog-eared postcard of Lima. I gave them some coins and told them to keep the card, but in a touching display of dignity they insisted I take it. These lads tore at my heartstrings. Instead of flowers at Sacha's funeral, I'd asked for donations to be made to a foundation for Colombian street kids. I realised, too late, that the nearby restaurant I'd dived into was full of wealthy Chinese who could afford its astronomical prices. I ordered a beer and the national dish of *ceviche*, a concoction of raw sea fish marinated in lemon and lime juice. Sacha had told me that Limeños took their food very seriously, and claimed it was the best cuisine in Latin America – if not the world. I found myself wondering what he'd made of the *ceviche* when he'd been in Peru eight years earlier.

Sacha had to spend several weeks in Lima because his passport and traveller's cheques were stolen. The theft coincided with my being in the Czech Republic, where there was no phone signal. American Express refused to replace the cheques until I'd verified his identity. I didn't pick up Sacha's calls until two weeks later.

He'd managed to survive, he later told me, because friends he'd made in Lima held a benefit for him. Whether it took place in an upmarket eatery like this or in a corrugated shack in the *barriadas* I hadn't a clue. It could have been either. He befriended people from all walks of life – unless, that is, they happened to be an authority figure or wore a uniform. For Sacha, being with almost anyone was preferable to being alone and at the mercy of the voices inside his head.

Back at El Balcón Dorado later that evening, I was in for a heart-stopping moment when I opened the door to my room. The bed had been made but my suitcase, containing my valuables, was lying brazenly unzipped in the middle of the floor. Trembling, I looked inside. Everything was still there, untouched, including my traveller's cheques. What an idiot! It was so unlike me, a seasoned traveller, to be that negligent. An early night was imperative. I hurried to a scruffy-looking café around the corner. Under cruel fluorescent lighting and the deafening screams and applause of non-Premier League football, I feasted, this time, on fried chicken, chips and Coca-Cola.

Prising open my hotel window I stared down at the stationary, toxic traffic below. The weather was damp, cloudy and cool – an unwelcome change from the sunshine of the day before. After waking up from a grief-laden dream and still incapable of making a decision about what I should do for the next month, my most sensible option, I realised, was to grab a cab and head for the Buddhist centre.

Hernan, the affable driver of my battered old Ford taxi, looked devastated when it conked out 30 seconds into the journey at a ferocious rush-hour junction. I had the feeling that this happened to him many times, on a daily basis, and that he was more concerned about losing my fare than with the deafening crescendo of angry horns. I got out and helped him push-start the car.

We managed, at last, to locate the Buddhist centre behind a high wall in the leafy, posh ambassadorial neighbourhood in the suburb of San Isidro. I pressed the entry phone. No answer.

To kill time before the centre opened – not that we knew when it would – we drove to the Huaca Pucllana – a massive pre-Inca adobe ruin nearby – but that, too, was closed. We drove on to the coastline at Miraflores, where the sea mist was so dense I couldn't see the sea. A wet, listless hour later we returned to the centre, only to find it was still closed. I felt a powerful surge of frustration; I needed to spiritually ground myself in Peru.

Hernan tried his hardest to convince me, as we headed back towards the city centre, that (for a substantial number of sol) I should let him spend the rest of the day driving me around the sights of Lima. We passed a vast concrete heap of a building, so hideous it made London's National Theatre look like the Alhambra Palace. I feigned interest when he told me it was the National Museum, and asked him to drop me off there. He smiled at me wistfully as we went our separate ways.

Once inside, I headed for the top floor, where there was an exhibition of ancient Peruvian gold artefacts. The spacious room I entered was completely dark and empty apart from a few illuminated exhibits of gold masks and trinkets. A museum guard in a green uniform insisted on following me around so closely I could feel his breath on the back of my neck.

When the Conquistadors arrived in Peru, Quechua was the official language of the Inca Empire, which was, at that time, the largest empire in the world. The guard told me his name was Ernesto, and that he was of Quechua descent – and proudly so. We chatted away in Spanish for a bit, and then he asked me how old I thought he was. Ernesto was easily 45 if a day – so I said 35 to be polite. He informed me – in all seriousness – that he was 27, and insisted on accompanying me all the way down multiple flights of stairs to the ground floor. We shook hands and he asked me for *uno besito* (a little kiss). I laughed and exclaimed '*Hombre! Non!*'

Downstairs, along with a handful of Latinos and Gringos, I was coaxed into joining the guided museum tour led by a Señor Ruiz. This bilingual, bespectacled 30-something guide had an extremely commanding voice – and no arms. He operated a torch with his teeth to illuminate designs on ancient Chavín and Nazca ceramics, and used his foot to draw explanatory diagrams of Moche pyramids and Wari sand settlements. His fascinating archaeological observations were interspersed with bouts of boyish, high-pitched giggling.

A couple from Ohio with teenage kids drifted away from the group when he told us that the Incas saw nothing wrong with having loads of sex, and then accused the Catholic Church of messing people's heads up over the centuries with its repressive morality. So he was brave, too. An outspoken comment like that, in such a deeply religious country, could cost Señor Ruiz his job.

I was riveted by the sheer energy of his performance – and by his humour. If he could triumph so cheerfully and unselfconsciously over such a disability, surely I could summon up the nerve to get out of Lima and see something of Peru?

Over lunch in the museum café, I made a few calls and managed to get hold of the number of the Buddhist centre in San Isidro. A warm voice answered the phone and assured me that the centre was now open.

Behind the impenetrably high wall at last, I was greeted by Oscar – a chubby young mestizo with sparkling brown eyes. He showed me around the spacious centre, where the utilitarian vibe was partially redeemed by an elegantly paved courtyard decked out with purple bougainvilleas and dwarf palms. As in all SGI (Value Creation Society) centres around the world there wasn't an orange robe or a shaven head in sight. This priest-free, socially engaged Buddhist organisation, based on the teachings of the 13th-century Buddhist teacher Nichiren Daishonin, believes in the universality of Buddhahood, and is a powerful peace movement and a United Nations NGO.

At my request, Oscar led me to the large, high-ceilinged chanting hall which contained several hundred fold-up chairs – and not a single person. For two hours I sat alone before the altar and chanted to the Peru Gohonzon: a mandala inscribed in black ink on a golden scroll that depicted in Sanskrit and ancient Chinese all the workings of life and the universe.

As I chanted, I remembered some of Sacha's fearless – and foolhardy – exploits in South America, such as travelling into the FARC guerrilla region in Colombia, a hotbed of kidnapping, to look for ancient Mayan ruins. Then I thought about the monks who never strayed from the cloisters of San Francisco Monastery, and of all the dried-up old bones lining the catacombs. And in my heart, I knew that Sacha would want me to see Peru. In fact, with his love of South America, he would smile and pronounce it 'wicked' that his ashes would be travelling around the country with me.

I made my way to Lima bus station, where I purchased a Royal Coach ticket to Cusco, with open stopping-off points on the way, on a coach departing the following morning. Then, in a retro travel agency near La Plaza Mayor, which had reams of carbon paper but not a computer or photocopier in sight, a young man called Luis spent nearly an hour on the phone booking my flight from Cusco back to Lima. His blonde highlights and earring-drooped earlobe were refreshingly out of place in the antediluvian agency. Outside, a noisy demonstration of people yelling '*Bastante! Bastante! Bastante!*' passed by.

I wondered what it was they'd had 'enough' of. '*Izquierdo o derecho?*' I asked Luis, curious to know whether the protesters were left-wing or right.

'*Centro derecho,*' Luis replied.

I took out my camera, hurried into the street and began snapping away. A jack-booted police officer in a dark grey uniform and matching baseball cap, clutching a riot shield, sprinted over to me and shook his baton in my face. I put my camera away and sloped off, reminding myself that sometimes I could be just as foolhardy as Sacha.

Before leaving Lima there was something I wanted to see. The cathedral was just around the corner from El Balcón Dorado, and inside it was Pizarro's tomb. The brightly coloured mosaic above his regal chapel neatly depicted the triumphs of Atahualpa's murderer: in the foreground, in full armour, Pizarro prayed with a clothed, converted Inca, while behind him a handful of Conquistadors herded naked Incas onto a rowing boat to be shipped off to Spain in an enormous galleon, its white sails billowing on the horizon.

I planted myself on a pew to admire the cathedral's voluptuous interior. Like their erstwhile Spanish conquerors, the Peruvians appeared to prefer sculptured mannequins in their churches to religious pictures. But the mannequins in this cathedral were unlike the grisly, bloodied, Madame Tussaud-like effigies I'd seen in Spanish churches. I gazed up in wonder at glittering life-sized Madonnas in ball gowns and virile, handsome young Christs.

Glancing up at the altar I discovered that I'd unwittingly become one of a congregation of eight. An elderly bishop in purple robes, aided by a young priest, was about to begin mass. Reluctant to reduce the bishop's minuscule flock even further, I resigned myself to sitting it out. As the mass murmured on, I watched a couple of baby-faced novices nervously dust the religious artefacts behind the altar. As a child, Sacha, too, had choirboy good looks. Would he still be alive, I wondered, if he'd been ugly?

The mass ended and I made my way out of the dimly-lit cathedral. It was Pizarro who had carried, on his shoulder, the first log to be used in the construction of the cathedral, and had laid its first stone. As I exited through the Portada del Perdón I hoped that, in an act of contrition, it was the treasure-thief himself who had named it the Gate of Forgiveness.